Test Your English

(With Vocabulary & Grammar Quiz for IELTS and All Competitive Exams)

Author
Dr. S. Venkatesh

DESCRIPTION

Title	:	Test Your English (With Vocabulary & Grammar Quiz for IELTS and All Competitive Exams)
Author	:	Dr. S. Venkatesh
Month & Year	:	September, 2023
Copyright	:	Dr. S. Venkatesh
Size	:	Demmy
ISBN	:	978-81-19337-81-1
Pages	:	104
Paper	:	Bookprint
Binding	:	Perfect Binding
Font size	:	11
Price	:	₹ 230.00
Publisher	:	Smt. SARASWATHY PUBLICATIONS Plot.62, Kalai Nagar, Near Tirunagar, Madurai - 625 006 (TN) Mail: vepsys@gmail.com Contact No: 9944097193

ACKNOWLEDGEMENT

I am immensely happy to publish my third book entitled **"Test Your English"**, which is meant for all learners of English in general, and those who are preparing for IELTS, TOEFL and other competitive exams, in particular.

I am very grateful to the **Hon'ble President, Vice President, Secretary, Treasurer, Board of Directors and Members of The Madura College Board** for their everlasting support and encouragement.

I express my hearty thanks to **Dr.J.Suresh, Principal, Heads of all departments Dr. Panneer Selvam, Chief Co-ordinator of SF Stream, faculties, non-teaching staff and all my beloved students** for their unstinting support to this noble cause.

I am indebted to all my family members and friends for their timely help to get this task completed in time.

Mr.Lakshmanan, Proprietor, and the team of Shanlax Publications are praised for the successful completion of this English language booster..

The notable feature of this book is that it is released on Teachers Day , 2023.

Dr.S.Venkatesh
Associate Professor of English,
The Madura College
Madurai-11.

99440 97193
vepsys@gmail.com

FOREWORD

Dear Readers,

It is my great pleasure to bring out my third book, **"Test Your English"**, which is very useful for all kinds of learners and aspirants of various competitive exams including IELTS, TOEFL, Bank Exams etc.,

I am indeed grateful to all the admirers and well wishers of my previous books, **'English For Elegance and Excellence' and 'Essential English and General Knowledge'**, published in 2020 and 2022 respectively.

This book, 'Test Your English' focuses on various useful topics including Sentence Formation, nitty gritty of English grammar, Vocabulary enrichment, Idioms & Phrases, Spot the errors and many other interesting and useful information.

It contains as many as1000 questions which are grouped into 10 sections with the answers given at the end of each.

One can test one's knowledge and proficiency in the language after solving this self-analytical test.

Your candid and valuable suggestions regarding the content and the presentation are solicited.

Thank you.

Dr.S.Venkatesh
Associate Professor of English,
The Madura College
Madurai-11.

99440 97193
vepsys@gmail.com

Dear readers,

Kindly watch my youtube channel, **"English for Elegance"** started on 22.01.2022 with over 65 short videos on Communicative English, Vocabulary Enrichment, Spot the Errors, Idioms and Phrases, etc.

So far 710 Subscribers ...

Viewers over 22,000 ...

Share and Subscribe to my channel,

"English for Elegance".

Some basic understanding of English

1. Avoid 'if' after 'suppose', 'in case' etc.,

eg: Suppose if you do this. (x)

Suppose you do this. (✓)

In case if you need money, (x)

In case you need money, (✓)

2. Don't use present perfect tense for definite past.

eg: He has completed his homework yesterday. (x)

He completed his homework yesterday. (✓)

3. Don't repeat the mistakes again and again. (x)

Don't repeat the mistakes. (or)

Don't commit the mistakes again and again. (✓)

4. I told to him that his job was good. (x)

I told him that his job was good. (✓)

5. Avoid using 'comma' after the words 'from' and 'to' in letter writing.

From,	(x)	From	(✓)
To,	(x)	To	(✓)

NOW, TRY YOUR ANSWERS

SECTION - A

Which of the following four is correct ?

1. The book was ________ to have been written by this author.
   a. supposedly b. supposed
   c. supposing d. suppose
2. Where did you ________ your belongings at the bus depot ?
   a. kept b. found c. left d. leave
3. All of a sudden, a ___________ smoke of gas erupted from the spot.
   a. huge b. thick c. enormous d. dangerous
4. Some children ____ have the habit of writing with left hand.
   a. are b. does c. do d. might
5. ___________ the fact that he is lazy, he is successful.
   a. Inspite of b. Despite c. Owing to d. Though
6. He was ____________ irregular in most of his duties.
   a. timely b. precisely c. never d. all ways
7. __________ attended the interview, she was confident of her success.
   a. After b. Having c. Immediately d. Only after
8. 'Never hesitate to help the needy' is a kind of _________.
   a. Requests b. Advice c. proverb d. Guiding
9. Even though he committed the crime, he ______ confessed.
   a. eagerly b. vehemently c. honestly d. mercilessly

10. Priya loves Carnatic music ______ her mother does.

a. so as b. as c. due to d. similarly

11. Don't leave any ________ on the right margin of the paper.

a. place b. margin c. space d. area

12. We ________ to follow the advice given by our elders.

a. have to b. should have c. must d. ought

13. Everyone of the students _________ a laptop with them.

a. had been b. are having c. have d. has

14. Each one rupee coin ________ around twenty five grams.

a. weigh b. weights c. weighs d. has

15. Optimism always leads to __________ steps.

a. progressive b. progress c. success d. successfull

16. The man's entry into the field was totally __________.

a. unlawfully b. unorganised

c. indecent d. unauthorized

17. ________ was the first maiden over in this IPL.

a. He's b. It's c. His d. That's

18. _________ knowing the truth, we are not supposed to judge.

a. Unless b. Not c. Unless d. Without

19. Several newspapers have __________ published this news.

a. all ready b. already c. repeated d. at time

20. 'People __________ in glass houses should not throw stones on others'.

a. who live b. lives c. living in d. who are

21. Out parents have been living in Mumbai ________ 2017.

a. from b. in c. before d. since

22. The road was _____ for nearly two hours due to heavy snow.

a. blacked b. effected c. stopped d. closed

23. Only after __________ the office, he remembered to close the window.

    a. leave b. leaving c. entering d. closed

24. "What for do you buy these expensive pens?", I____ her.

    a. asked b. asked to c. told d. was asked

25. Many countries are ___________of this agreement.

    a. Signatories b. Signatures c. Signing d. to sign

26. You all should do this work___________.

    a. yourself b. yourselves c. yourself's d. yourselve's

27. Unable to cope ________ the situation, he resigned the job.

    a. up with b. up c. with d. for

28. The teacher said that the earth __________ around the Sun.

    a. resolves b. revolved c. revolves d. is revolving

29. You have taken the right decision, ___________you ?

    a. aren't b. have not c. have d. haven't

30. A number of students ________ visiting the Botanical Garden on sunday.

    a. have been b. will have c. will been d. will be

31. Mala managed to draw a circle _______ the help of a bangle.

    a. by b. using c. with out d. with

32. The exact number of visitors to the park today _______ 209.

    a. is b. are c. nearly d. above

33. Where did you _______ this application form ?

    a. got b. sent c. have got d. get

34. In case ______ you read the letter twice, you will know its contents.

    a. if b. of

    c. may d. nothing required

35. Shyamala drove the car easily, __________ she ?

a. does b. did c. didn't d. wasn't

36. ______________ speaking, English is a wonderful language.

a. Roughly b. Personally c. Technically d. Firstly

37. Are you sure that the flight was late ______ 30 minutes ?

a. for b. more than c. into d. by

38. _______ the lion chased the deer, the photographer shot this.

a. As b. During c. Before d. Rarely

39. For the first time, a woman Prime Minister ______ the nation.

a. greated b. greeting c. addressed d. address

40. He has been ________ several times not to play on roadsides

a. warning b. warns c. warned d. suggested

41. The pen drive that you __________ yesterday is found here.

a. last b. forgotten c. had lost d. misplaced

42. When the index finger points _____ the moon, the idiot looks at the finger.

a. out b. at c. out d. for

43. It was ________ who spoke brilliantly in the meeting.

a. Him b. he c. himself d. his

44. How many of them ________ interested in learning English?

a. have b. is c. are d. was

45. We did the homework ___________ using a computer.

a. ourself b. our selves c. ourselves d. ourself's

46. Geetha found the book ____________ near the study room.

a. somewhere b. some where c. anywhere d. everywhere

47. The new typist ___________ committed the mistakes again and again.

a. repeated b. repeatedly c. unknowing d. none

48. The team batting second was ____________ the target.

a. anywhere b. nowhere c. no near d. nearly

49. If you had worked hard, you __________ scored better.

a. would've b. can have c. might be d. will have

50. The reason why he comes late is he misses the bus ________.

a. today b. hardly ever c. some time d. frequently

51. ________ Day is celebrated on November 14th every year.

a. Childrens b. Childrens' c. Children's d. Children's'

52. We have to give ___________ importance to learn English.

a. utmost b. atmost c. ut most d. fully

53. Speak the truth, ____________ you will be punished.

a. if don't b. if not c. otherwise d. other wise

54. Where ____________ you stay last night ?

a. did do b. was c. were d. did

55. Call me __________ you reach your hostel.

a. Ones b. once at c. one's d. once

56. There was an emergency meeting to discuss ____ the issue.

a. about b. on c. with d. none

57. "To err is human", is a very popular ____________.

a. message b. quote c. proverb d. information

58. The total number of students in the camp at present ___ 179.

a. are b. is c. has been d. over

59. If you had gone in time, you _________ caught the train.

a. could b. would c. would've d. might

60. Excuse me. _________ you please assist me now?

a. May b. Could c. Will d. Might

61. The new bridge was constructed _________ the river.

a. across b. on c. under d. besides

62. Neither the story nor the poem is __________ by the teacher.
    a. teaches b. not teaching c. taught d. covering
63. An emergency meeting ____ by the District administration.
    a. will conduct b. was convene
    c. was drawn d. was convened
64. What were you ___________ when I called you ?
    a. done b. did c. doing d. do
65. Don't enter the class room ____________ your ID cards.
    a. with out b. barring c. using d. without
66. Leave sufficient __________ between each question.
    a. place b. page c. space d. gape
67. The money lender was ______ greedy to collect the interest.
    a. as over as b. much c. more d. excessively
68. Which of the three portraits _______ newly bought?
    a. has been b. are being c. have d. have been
69. __________ read the book, he took some break.
    a. Have had b. Having c. To have d. After
70. It is a ____________ in his academic career.
    a. landmark b. milestone's
    c. achievement d. feather cap
71. I couldn't find my dog __________ near the gate.
    a. nowhere b. anywhere c. somewhere d. closely
72. The school children shouted _________ against drug abuse.
    a. voices b. opposition c. slogans d. placards
73. In case _________ you wish to apply for the job, do it now.
    a. if b. do c. of d. none
74. During your school days you got distinction, _______ you ?
    a. were b. did not c. aren't you d. didn't

75. All the questions in this part are interesting,__________?

a. isn't it b. aren't it c. haven't it d. aren't they

76. We have to overcome our difficulties by using our_______.

a. knowledge b. interest c. power d. will power

77. The marriage took place between 8 am ________ 9 am in Cochin.

a. to b. and c. till d. before

78. He was very much__________in the hospital yesterday.

a. conscience b. confidence c. slept d. conscious

79. Gupta as well as his sister________a tall student.

a. is b. are c. has d. have

80. We have to educate children to________poverty.

a. balance b. chase c. remove d. eradicate

81. He asked me what __________then.

a. I did b. I was did c. I had done d. I was doing

82. Due to _______of funds, the meeting was cancelled.

a. demote b. deficit c. insufficient d. lacking

83. It rained cats and_______in our city last night.

a. rats b. mouses c. dog's d. dogs

84. Shyam, a cousin___________of mine, is an auditor.

a. brother b. brother's c. relative d. none

85. "The______of the temple is fantastic!", the foreigner said.

a. beauty b. tower's c. entrances d. architecture

86. How many of them are___________in today's meeting?

a. attend b. willing c. presented d. present

87. __________people are smart enough in using cell phones.

a. Now a day's b. Nowadays

c. Nowadays' d. Most of

88. He wanted to learn English when he was a / an __________.

a. childhood b. young c. adolescent d. reader

89. The Indian bowlers __________ more runs in the last 5 overs.

a. concealed b. conceded c. conquered d. donated

90. Ninety per cent of the population of the village ________ literates.

a. has been b. is being c. have d. are

91. "Necessity is the ______ of invention" is a famous proverb.

a. Mother b. father c. beginning d. mother

92. In all __________ they are going to change the syllabus.

a. formality b. likelihood c. promptness d. likely hood

93. This book, of course, is more _______ than that of the other.

a. interested b. interestful c. easier d. interesting

94. The other name for 'last but one' is ______________.

a. fag end b. near last c. penultimate d. peculiar

95. The Manager called ______ the Director regarding some key issues.

a. off b. to c. on d. into

96. The ________ in our city today is really pleasant.

a. weather b. whether c. climate d. atmosphere

97. As the work was ________ I had to stay in the office longer.

a. incomplete b. heavily c. discontinued d. endlessly

98. Kindly pay attention to what _________.

a. he say's b. he said c. he says d. he told

99. All these books are mine ; not _________.

a. yours b. your's c. them d. their's

100. Kindly let me know once he returns _______ from Mumbai.

a. back b. soon c. suddenly d. none

Answers

1.	b	2.	d	3.	b	4.	c	5.	b
6.	c	7.	b	8.	b	9.	c	10.	b
11.	c	12.	d	13.	d	14.	c	15.	a
16.	d	17.	c	18.	d	19.	b	20.	a
21.	d	22.	d	23.	b	24.	a	25.	a
26.	b	27.	c	28.	c	29.	d	30.	d
31.	d	32.	a	33.	d	34.	d	35.	c
36.	b	37.	d	38.	a	39.	c	40.	c
41.	d	42.	b	43.	b	44.	c	45.	c
46.	a	47.	d	48.	b	49.	a	50.	d
51.	c	52.	a	53.	c	54.	d	55.	d
56.	d	57.	b	58.	b	59.	c	60.	b
61.	a	62.	c	63.	d	64.	c	65.	d
66.	c	67.	d	68.	a	69.	b	70.	a
71.	b	72.	c	73.	d	74.	d	75.	d
76.	d	77.	b	78.	d	79.	a	80.	d
81.	d	82.	b	83.	d	84.	d	85.	d
86.	d	87.	b	88.	c	89.	b	90.	d
91.	d	92.	b	93.	d	94.	c	95.	c
96.	a	97.	a	98.	c	99.	a	100.	d

Your score now ____/100

SECTION - B

Which of the following four is correct ?

101. Every parent was asked to sit on __________ allotted seats.
a. his b. an c. theirs d. their

102. Take the umbrella with you as it is __________.
a. raining b. rained c. rain's d. rains

103. As soon as the Collector came, the meeting ____________.
a. has started b. was started c. started soon d. begun

104. Before ____ the questions, read the instructions thoroughly.
a. answering b. answered c. you answer d. answers

105. As he wasted most of his time, he is _________ now.
a. toiling b. trialling c. thrilling d. failure

106. Due to the ___ of the main batsmen, the team lost the match.
a. carelessness b. pour batting
c. neglect d. negligent

107. Don't go _________ without informing me.
a. any where b. anywhere c. nowhere d. somewhere

108. The ambulance driver suddenly __________ the break .
a. stopped b. holded c. handled d. applied

109. The distance between Madurai and Chennai ________ nearly 500 kms..
a. are b. has been c. is d. is only

110. Sangeetha ____________ typewriting at a very young age.
a. had learnt b. learnt c. known d. practicing

111. __________ but the rich can buy that expensive bungalow.
a. All b. Everyman c. None d. Except

112. No sooner did he ________ the dog than he ran away.
a. watched b. see c. approach d. meet

113. Sachin is better than __________ cricketer in India.
a. no other's b. all others c. any other d. many other

114. He is honest ________ he is very poor.
a. despite b. inspite of c. all though d. although

115. Before opening the letter, _________ it belongs to you.
a. insure b. conform c. assure d. ensure

116. Asha came late. ____________ she got the attendance.
a. Moreover b. How ever c. Although d. However

117. __________ chapter of the book is very interesting.
a. A sixth b. Sixth c. 6th d. The sixth

118. Meena and her sister ____________ their mother.
a. resembles like b. resembling
c. resemble d. looks like

119. While making sentences, he committed ________ mistakes.
a. mostly b. a lot of c. all d. some of

120. The talks between the leaders took place ____ high security.
a. in b. with c. surrounding d. amidst

121. This shop contains all sorts of ___________ items.
a. stationary b. stationery c. stationeries d. eating

122. It was the __________ wicket for the bowler on his debut.
a. maidan b. initial c. maiden d. beginning

123. It was a _________ fantastic speech by the Prime Minister.
a. very b. more c. much d. none

124. The work was done earlier than ___________.
a. last date b. dead line c. said d. expected

125. The reason for this ________ delay is frequent power cuts.
a. excess b. inordinate c. unduly d. overseen

126. The actor was awarded ____________ last year.

a. lately b. recently
c. some how d. posthumously

127. The flight was suddenly ____________ due to bad weather.

a. reaching b. was landed c. stopped d. landed

128. Do you know how many of them ______ English fluently ?

a. speaks b. can speak
c. can be speaking d. speak to

129. ____________ is one of the major causes of suffering.

a. over thinking b. overthinking
c. overthought d. overthink

130. Geetha's ____________ is her cousin Mala.

a. confident b. confidant c. confidence d. Company

131. The past participle of 'direct' is ____________.

a. direction b. directly c. directing d. directed

132. The noun form of 'deny' is ____________.

a. deniel b. denial c. denied d. dening

133. The incorrect suffix to the word 'refuse' is __________.

a. refusing b. refraisal c. refusal d. refused

134. It is Sunil's ___________ now to take down the notes.

a. round b. choice c. turn d. chance

135. He has been told _________ times not to repeat the mistake.

a. lot b. umpteen c. many a d. much of

136. This little boy can __________ the sounds of various birds.

a. execute b. practice c. imitate d. modulate

137. There was a __________ contest for the post of President.

a. neck b. full c. closest d. stiff

138. Underline the __________ given in the following passage.
a. phonetics b. sentences c. words d. gerunds

139. Did you __________ the money before leaving the counter ?
a. counting b. counted c. cheque d. count

140. It was Swetha, not ____________ who came here last week.
a. his cousin b. nobody c. her sister d. anybody

141. I find this book very __________ to read.
a. interested b. interestly c. interesting d. Interestingly

142. The spectators lost their _______ when the team was about to lose.
a. hopeful b. dream c. charm d. interest

143. "Men may come and Men may go " is a famous __________.
a. argument b. statement c. poetic line d. finding

144. The paper was _________ into pieces by the child.
a. turn b. teared c. tore d. torn

145. The opposite of the word 'appropriate' is ____ appropriate.
a. semi b. un c. dis d. in

146. The adverb among the following words is ___________.
a. joyful b. fastly c. lily d. fast

147. Which of the following is a negative expression ?
a. neitherly b. seldom c. failure d. but

148. Your books are there, ___________ ?
a. isn't it b. are not c. is it not d. aren't they

149. If you want to be successful, ________ people's comments.
a. cope up with b. withstood
c. agree d. ignore

150. The reason for his _______ late is, he missed the college bus.
a. entering b. actual c. come d. coming

151. The word 'procrastination' means __________.
  a. delay b. failure c. prevent d. introduce

152. The teacher said, "________ comes late, will be punished."
  a. who ever b. whenever c. Whom so ever d. Whoever

153. The diary ___________ of more than 200 pages.
  a. comprises b. consist c. contains d. consists

154. ___________ he spoke well is a sign of his progress in communication.
  a. If b. When c. Suppose d. That

155. Don't spread rumours even ____________.
  a. by mistake b. anywhere c. nowhere d. outside

156. The cabinet ______________ agreed to the resolution.
  a. vehemently b. fully
  c. regularly d. unanimously

157. I wish I _______________ a little bird.
  a. have b. was c. were d. might be

158. Dilip is ______________ of some principles in Physics.
  a. ignorance b. innocent c. ignorant d. awareness

159. As soon as the Revenue Officials came, the ___ was started.
  a. enquiries b. enquiry c. debate d. orders

160. This is Mano ___________ I have bought this phone.
  a. for whom b. whom c. whose d. for him

161. Degrees of comparison is used in Adjectives and ________.
  a. Prepositions b. Verbs c. Phrases d. Adverbs

162. He leaned ______________ the wall to gain support.
  a. under b. within c. nearly d. on

163. Interview is a ____________ to test one's overall ability.
  a..platfarm b. platform c. place d. opportunity

164. The _________ numbers of 11 are 12, 13, 14 etc.,

a. succeedingly b. succeeding

c. continued d. next

165. What part of speech is ' myself' ?

a. Noun b. adjective c. Pro noun d. pronoun

166. He stood __________ when he was chased by the dogs.

a. wrongly b. help less c. aghast d. curious

167. The ________ bus collided with the truck suddenly.

a. unlucky b. ill-fated

c. mischievous d. overcrowd

168. Harish knows English ________ than his friends do.

a. more b. better c. higher d. superior

169. In the event of your __________ first, I will give a treat.

a. application b. come c. came d. scoring

170. Listening is one of the most _______ communicative skills.

a. interesting b. commonly c. important d. easiest

171. The umpire _____ the match due to unpredictable weather.

a. refused b. called off c. cancelled off d. took off

172. How many of you __________ this movie for the first time ?

a. seeing b. have watched

c. seen d. watching

173. As she was very ______, she was praised by her colleagues.

a. punctually b. peculiar c. prompted d. punctual

174. Our relatives from abroad may ____ come here tomorrow.

a. perhaps b. have c. likely d. none

175. Never ______________ your opponents: it's a warning .

a. under estimate b. unestimate

c. overestimate d. underestimate

176. It was a / the ____________ unique photo of Gandhiji.

a. most b. rarer c. rarest d. none

177. Several participants ___________ from the contest later.

a. withdraw b. withdrawn c. withdrew d. removed

178. The __________ capacity of this water tank is 1000 litres.

a. higher b. fully c. nearly d. maximum

179. 'Between the deep sea and the ________' is a famous idiom.

a. dragon b. ghost c. devil d. cobra

180. _____ you pay the remaining fees, you can't get hall ticket.

a. If b. if not c. Unless d. In case you not

181. The terrorists ______ country-made bombs on the vehicles.

a. throwed b. thrown c. put d. hurled

182. His only plan is to win the election by hook or __________.

a. loop b. force c. brook d. crook

183. The candidate ___________ the win by the highest margin.

a. register b. received c. got d. registered

184. Sleep is a ______________ death for any man.

a. temporary b. remedial c. immediate d. natural

185. I have never seen such an ____________ response ever.

a. overall of b. over estimate

c. overwhelming d. overly

186. There is no ____________ for his survival now.

a. likely hood b. probabile c. expectation d. scope

187. 'Cash for vote' is a / an____ for any kind of election.

a. unwanted b. unseen c. threat d. boon

188. The boat was ______________ by the cyclone yesterday.

a. removed b. washed c. broked d. capsized

189. Gupta's ancestors ____________ here many decades ago.
    a. lived b. have lived
    c. have been living d. were lived
190. The singer ____________ the audience by her sweet voice.
    a. arises b. enthralled c. affected d. shocked
191. The ____________ of the book is really wonderful.
    a. wrappers b. wrapper c. wropper d. wraper
192. "Appearances are always __________" is a famous proverb.
    a. deceive b. receptive c. deceptive d. misleading
193. They could see the tower __________ the square hole.
    a. off b. through c. from d. in
194. The ______________ was poor due to heavy mist.
    a. road b. visible c. vision d. visibility
195. Though he was ___________ nobody criticized him.
    a. alerted b. accurate
    c. accomplished d. unscrupulous
196. Sholay was one of the greatest hits of ______________.
    a. past time b. longstanding
    c. yesteryear d. ever
197. You don't like coffee, ___________?
    a. is it b. do you c. don't you d. aren't you
198. Preethi is always cut and ________ in her speech.
    a. tried b. correct c. right d. dried
199. Vinodh is partially hearing __________.
    a. impaired b. effected c. lost d. trouble
200. The best medicine for good health is ____________.
    a. happy b. be happy c. laughter d. worriless

Answers

101. d 102. a 103. b 104. a 105. a
106. a 107. b 108. d 109. c 110. b
111. c 112. b 113. c 114. d 115. d
116. d 117. d 118. c 119. b 120. d
121. b 122. c 123. d 124. d 125. b
126. d 127. d 128. b 129. b 130. b
131. d 132. b 133. b 134. c 135. b
136. c 137. d 138. d 139. d 140. c
141. c 142. d 143. c 144. d 145. d
146. d 147. b 148. d 149. d 150. d
151. a 152. d 153. d 154. d 155. a
156. d 157. c 158. c 159. b 160. a
161. d 162. d 163. b 164. b 165. d
166. c 167. b 168. b 169. d 170. c
171. b 172. b 173. d 174. d 175. d
176. d 177. c 178. d 179. c 180. c
181. d 182. d 183. d 184. a 185. c
186. d 187. c 188. d 189. a 190. b
191. b 192. c 193. b 194. d 195. d
196. c 197. b 198. d 199. a 200. c

Your score now ___/100

SECTION - C

Which of the following four is correct ?

201. The hospital wore a ____ look after the VIP was discharged.
   a. deserted b. blank c. empty d. vacant
202. He has been ____________ many a time not to smoke.
   a. said b. adviced c. threatened d. advised
203. It is really difficult to part ___________ the pet animals.
   a. off b. away c. without d. with
204. The ______________ to the meeting was very poor today.
   a. attendence b. gatherings c. visitors d. attendance
205. Had you ______ been my friend, I would not have advised.
   a. never b. ever c. no d. not
206. The Insurance company called him for _______________.
   a. suspection b. suspiscion c. lending d. verification
207. Mrs. Deepa holds a _________ role in this office.
   a. duel b. double c. dual d. differing
208. We decided to ______ the meeting due to personal reasons.
   a. withheld b. with hold c. refer d. defer
209. The Lok Sabha was adjourned __________ by the Speaker.
   a. Unanimously b. sine-die
   c. recently d. lastly
210. The _____________ to the election was over yesterday.
   a. campaigning b. formalities
   c. conduct d. forms
211. I know that he is the _______________ brother of the three.
   a. senior b junior c. latest d. youngest

212. Neither the relatives nor the neighbours ________________ to him.

a. opposing b. helped c. spoke d. aware of

213. Parking is ___________ in this area due to the local festival.

a. prevented b. disallowed

c. not acceptance d. unaloud

214. This is Mr. Mukesh ________ sisters are working in Cochin.

a. who's b. whom c. whose's d. whose

215. ____________ pollution is a big threat nowadays.

a. noisy b. Noise c. Sound's d. Chemical's

216. The antonym of 'famous' is __________.

a. disfamous b. imfamous c. unifamous d. infamous

217. The government passed an ___________ in the parliament.

a. ordinance b. ordnance c. settlement d truce

218. The adverb of ' responsibility' is ________________.

a. responsively b. responsibly

c. responsibily d. respectively

219. " ____________ favours the brave " is a famous quote.

a. friendship b. fight c. finish d. fortune

220. His ____________ in English language is stupendous.

a. accurately b. capacity c. proficiency d. glorious

221. It was ________, not his uncle who signed the document.

a. he b. his' c. him d. himself

222. ____________ the above circumstances, he availed leave.

a. Due b. For c. According to d. Under

223. Quite a few of my relatives are working ________ abroad.

a. in b. on c. from d. none

224. You posted the letter yesterday, ____________ ?

a. did you b. are you c. isn't it d. didn't you

225. Where __________ you when I phoned you ?

a. was b. did c. had d. were

226. The __________ today is extremely pleasant.

a. whether b. climate c. forecast d. weather

227. The PM's visit was __________ on all the news channels.

a. telecast b. broad casted c. relied d. relaid

228. What part of speech is the word, 'ineffective' ?

a. noun b. adverb c. antonym d. adjective

229. We all should try to __________ poverty at any cost.

a. admonish b. eradicate c. exempt d. execute

230. His behavior is __________ from many other students'.

a. peculiar b. more peculiar

c. different d. more different.

231. Remove the bad __________ from the basket immediately.

a. one's b. once c. once' d. ones

232. The parliament witnessed __________ pandemonium.

a. unpresidented b. unpresident

c. unrulingly d. unprecedented

233. Vinodh is not an expert; he is merely a ____________.

a. waste b. coach c. mediocre d. mediocer

234. As there was noise ____________, I went out to study.

a. every where b. somewhere

c. nowhere d. everywhere

235. His success was __________ due to the role of media.

a. achieved b. untoward c. highlighted d. greatest

236. He gave _____ his bad habits because of his friend's advice.

a. away   b. down   c. off   d. up

237. Don't distract my __________ while driving.

a. sights   b. views   c. concentrate   d. attention

238. All his ________ are in fine condition, according to the scan.

a. entrails   b. body's organ

c. conditions   d. parts

239. This match is, as of now, ________________.

a. equally ready   b. evenly poised

c. balanced   d. unpredicting

240. Sneha never behaved ____________ anytime.

a. responsefully   b. responsible

c. irresponsibly   d. irreasonably

241. All the candidates ____________ to enter the hall at 2 pm.

a. allowed   b. was allowed

c. have been allowed   d. were allowed

242. The manager asked me whether I _________ shorthand.

a. know   b. knew

c. am knowing   d. known

243. "How many of them ____________ the hall tickets so far" ?

a. received   b. have received

c. got   d. uploaded

244. Whenever I visit my ______________ I greet my teachers.

a. almameter   b. almanmater

c. ex-schooling   d. alma mater

245. Vinitha spoke brilliantly on the _____________ of smoking.

a. effects   b. pros and corns

c. pros and cons   d. dismerits

246. There is no ____________ to anyone for the tour.

a. exception b. freedom c. chance d. diversion

247. The traffic police _____ the flow of vehicles due to accident.

a. diversed b. changed c. diverged d. diverted

248. Be quiet ________ the news comes from the Head quarters.

a. unless b. when c. until d. untill

249. The ___________ of the criminals are not yet known.

a. hide b. location

c. where abouts d. whereabouts

250. Due to ________ of time, I could not attend all the questions.

a. paucity b. shortages c. pausity d. running

251. As I had a ____________ nose, I felt uncomfortable.

a. running b. sneeze c. poor d. runny

252. The adverb of 'Quality' is __________________.

a. qualitative b. qualification

c. qualitively d. qualitatively

253. Mr. Sundar is __________ in all his dealings.

a. uprighted b. straightforward

c. punctually d. promptly

254. Are you able to understand the ______ behind this move ?

a. rational b. logical c. logician d. rationale

255. Never try to _______ his image, as he is a very good person.

a. downsize b. belittle c. be little d. low

256. The Manager was __________ to issue such warning letters.

a. happily b. sure

c. constrained d. overwhelmed

257. I saw a ____________ old poor boy at the meeting.

a. ten year b. ten years c. smaller d. ten year's

258. He was punished for his ___________ of duty in the office.

a. negligent b. deny c. refuse d. negligence

259. Did you ___ any word against the functioning of the Trust ?

a. speech b. made c. utter d. told

260. He " kicked the bucket" means, he ____________.

a. dead b. fell down c. was angry d. died

261. He _______________ aware of the consequences.

a. was no b. wasn't c. didn't d. couldn't

262. Pradip is ________________ than any other actors.

a. more prettier b. handsomely

c. rather costly d. more handsome

263. It is our duty to _______ the sovereignty of our constitution.

a. withhold b. uphold c. consider d. evaluate

264 The house owner demanded more money for the _________ charges.

a. maintaining of b. maintenance

c. managing d. developing

265. _____________ of the ill effects, he consumed liquor

a. Knowing b. Un mindful c. Unmindfull d. Unmindful

266. Please wait here ________________ he returns from office.

a. until b. unless c. since d. when

267. He has to ________ at least a little knowledge of computer.

a. has b. had c. having d. have

268. The road show was conducted by the Rotaract Club ______.

a. sincerely b. recently c. soon d. pastly

269. We require a / an ________ amount of money to complete the project.

a. furtherly b. greatest c. largest d. enormous

270. While reading ________ the lines, I understood the hidden meaning.

a. through b. along c. between d. down

271. A __________ share of the work was done by Mrs. Sudha.

a. hill's b. camel's c. lion's d. line's

272. The citizens exercised their _________ responsibly.

a. vote's b. poll c. franchise d. election

273. The meeting was __________ due to the bad weather.

a. put on b. put out c. deferred d. convened

274. Almost all the parties try to ______ voters during elections.

a. plead b. request c. compel d. allure

275. Some of your friends are doctors, ______________?

a. isn't it b. don't they c. do they d. aren't they

276. India has developed __________ since its independence.

a. manifold b. many a fold c. immense d. fastly

277. Do you wish to meet the manager ___________?

a. quickly b. soon c. latter d. urgently

278. If you want to succeed, _________ your negative thoughts.

a. deleted b. educate c. shun d. abolish

279. The Principal's absence was __________ in the meeting.

a. known b. debate

c. significant d. conspicuous

280. The ___________ of the stolen painting are unknown.

a. locality b. place

c. location d. whereabouts

281. The power supply was __________ though it was raining.

a. interrupted b. maintaining

c. complete d. uninterrupted

282. As his performance was ____________, the audience applauded.

a. amazed b. extra ordinary
c. exceptionally d. extraordinary

283. As the difference was so ____________, we couldn't feel it.

a. leant b. thinning c. lowly d. subtle

284. Isn't there ______ to receive petition from this old woman ?

a. anyone b. no one c. someone d. any one's

285. The __________ report shows it was an accidental death.

a. post meridian b. postmartemed
c. autopsy d. biological

286. Dilip ran from __________ to post to get the job done.

a. post b. dot c. over d. pillar

287. Finish your program. We are ______ short of time.

a. away b. less c. already d. running

288. "Between the deep sea and the ____________", is an idiom.

a. forest b. river c. hell d. devil

289. The ___________ were asked to sit at the front.

a. awardies b. participant's c. awarderss d. awardees

290. Manisha has a ________ good speed to work on computers.

a. awareness b. reasonably c. superb d. reasonable

291. The _________ was so high that the farmers felt very happy.

a. agriculture b. sowing c. fertile d. harvest

292. In the event of your ___________ you will get more pride.

a. elected b. succeed c. promoting d. success

293. The bank _________ carry out any transactions on holidays.

a. is not b. do not c. does not d. may not

294. ________ his laziness, he completes all his works promptly.

a. Owing to b. In spite of c. Inspite off d. Though

295. I may need your moral support ______________.

a. every times b. everytime c. at times d. at time

296. As he was in a state of __________, he forgot his address.

a. pavilion b. oblivion c. obvious d. shocking

297. You are not __________ to do this without my knowledge.

a. excused b. suppose c. let d. supposed

298. ______________ is the opposite of being valiant.

a. coward b. braveness c. cowardice d. cowardise

299. No one could enter the building as it was ______________.

a. destructed b. destroyed

c. for away d. dilapidated

300. Priya asked Harish when the textile shop ____________.

a. will open b. opened c. would open d. be opened

Answers

201. a 202. d 203. d 204. d 205. d
206. d 207. c 208. d 209. b 210. a
211. d 212. c 213. b 214. d 215. b
216. d 217. a 218. b 219. d 220. c
221. a 222. d 223. d 224. d 225. d
226. d 227. a 228. d 229. b 230. c
231. d 232. d 233. c 234. d 235. c
236. d 237. d 238. a 239. b 240. c
241. d 242. b 243. b 244. d 245. c
246. a 247. d 248. c 249. d 250. a
251. d 252. d 253. b 254. d 255. b
256. c 257. a 258. d 259. c 260. d
261. b 262. d 263. b 264. b 265. d
266. a 267. d 268. b 269. d 270. c
271. c 272. c 273. c 274. d 275. d
276. a 277. d 278. c 279. d 280. d
281. d 282. d 283. d 284. a 285. c
286. d 287. d 288. d 289. d 290. d
291. d 292. d 293. c 294. b 295. c
296. b 297. d 298. c 299. d 300. c

Your score now ___ / 100

SECTION - D

Which of the following four is correct ?

301. They fought ' ________ and nail' to win the match.
   a. iron b. hammer c. wall d. tooth

302. The __________ of the temple was beautifully made.
   a. copy b. structural c. designs d. replica

303. We have placed orders for the _________ of our Manager's signature.
   a. duplicate b. facksimile c. facsimile d. fakesimile

304. We purchased 'all and ____ ' for the proposed programme.
   a. all b. every c. out d. sundry

305. You will accompany us to the hall , ___________ ?
   a. wont you b. will you c. won't you d. can you

306. He __________ his crime honestly in the court .
   a. confused b. admited c. conferred d. confessed

307. Brinda is _________ than most of her friends.
   a. more taller b. as tall c. tallest d. taller

308. While __________ the car, he concentrated on the road.
   a. drove b. driving c. travelling d. halting

309. Go and take the book __________ you want.
   a. whatever b. whichever c. which ever d. in case if

310. His wealth was ______________ to his earnings.
   a. more than b. greater
   c. disproportionate d. disloyal

311. Don't talk ___________ , as the child is sleeping.
   a. allowed b. much c. loud d. aloud

312. His grandfather had settled the land issue ______ his death.

a. during b. at c. after d. before

313. He is 'a cat on the wall' means, he is ____________.

a. negative b. indecisive c. irregular d. indecided

314. There was not even a / an _____ of doubt about his honesty.

a. iota b. iyoyta c. inch d. little

315. The team lacked the _______ for the tour, so it cancelled it.

a. whereupon b. funding

c. wherewithals d. wherewithal

316. The term ' par excellence' means _______________ .

a. average b. better than a few

c. better than all d. oldest

317. The patient walks _________ after the treatment.

a. fastly b. quickly c. languidly d. lonely

318. His statement is _______________, as he is misleading.

a. bilateral b. bilingual c. confusing d. ambiguous

319. The MP _________ bungalow is here, is a learned man.

a. whom b. who is c. which d. whose

320. Meena and Arthy are sisters. The ___________ is taller.

a. later b. letter c. farmer d. latter

321. It was _________ that he was not selected for the post.

a. unjust b. injust c. unluck d. cruelty

322. Earlier he had applied for the post of Manager _____ times.

a. umpteen b. most c. various' d. number of

323. It is believed that ______ is the root cause of all the troubles.

a. lazy b. Truth c. Failure d. Avarice

324. The court issued ___________ to him repeatedly.

a. reports b. summonses c. summon d. warning's

325. They depended on ____________ during the exams.

a. others' b. themselves c. themself d. ours

326. Kindly pay least attention to ____________ matters.

a. serious b. trivial c. personal d. umpteen

327. It was his ____________ part that he rejected the best offer.

a. disrespect b. immovable c. insincere d. negligent

328. ________________ he comes to the college very late.

a. sometime b. sometimes' c. some times' d. occasionally

329. ____________ to emerging protest, the bank reinstated him.

a. Agreeing b. Owing c. Accepting d. Acceding

330. As the series is already won, this match is ____________.

a. unconsequential b. inconsequential

c. waste d. uninterested

331. The terrorists were caught ____________ by the Army.

a. blue handed b. iron handed

c. gradually d. red handed

332. Sneha donated goods to the ____________ recently.

a. orphionage b. orphans'

c. orphan ages d. orphanage

333. The suffix for the word 'address' is ________________.

a. ee b. addressee c. addresses d. addressing

334. I started my morning walk at 6 am ____________ today.

a. in the morning b. this morning

c. for this d. none

335. Meena ____________ to my invitation through telephone.

a. respected b. respond c. reciprocated d. replayed

336. Despite her resounding success, Yogasri was ___________.

a. simple b. humble c. sincere d. polite

337. The employee's medical expenses _______ by the company.

a. beared b. were given c. was borne d. were borne

338. He was a / an __________ against corruption in our office.

a. epitome b. roll model c. example d. expert

339. Don't tell the full story as we need just the ____________.

a. summary b. result

c. short d. quintessence

340. The PM's speech was __________ on TV yesterday.

a. telecast b. telecasted c. listened d. shared

341. It was a/ an really ______ dinner arranged by our college.

a. famous b. mouthwater c. mega's d. sumptuous

342. This document is mine. Where is __________ ?

a. your's b. yours' c. your other d. yours

343. As he was always ______________, he never felt happy.

a. contentiously b. unsatisfied

c. insatiable d. avarice

344. 'We love a thing when we fear its ____________'.

a. lost b. lass c. missing d. loss

345. ____________ persons are not allowed inside auditorium.

a. Unknowned b. Unseen

c. Unwanted d. Unauthorized

346. The cause of the accident is yet to be _____________.

a. ascertained b. understood c. awaited d. received

347. Without ____________ you cannot get a seat in this college..

a. enrolement b. advancement c. permission d. enrollment

348. He got ready with all his __________ before the interview.

a. files b. marks sheets

c. credentials d. achievements

349. Sandeep sent the application at the ____________ hour.

a. lost b. last c. final d. eleventh

350. The office opens at 10 am, ____________ ?

a. isn't it b. does it c. wont it d. doesn't it

351. I gave the __________ a pair of old pants last week.

a. ruffain b. needer c. people d. mendicant

352. The _________ of the people is more important nowadays.

a. vox populi b. sentiments c. verdict d. comments

353. The participants who ____ their names , can assemble here.

a. enrolls b. enrollment

c. have enrolled d. enroll

354. No sooner __________ he come, than all of us stood up.

a. when b. once c. does d. did

355. The temple authorities allowed all the _______ one by one.

a. pedestrians b. people c. participants d. devotees

356. Sivaji Ganesan's acting is always ________________.

a. magic b. greatest c. inimitable d. wonder

357. Sachin never gave any chance ____________ his innings.

a. full off b. through out c. full of d. throughout

358. Let's not discuss _________ this matter now.

a. about b. on c. over d. none

359. His penury ____________ him to seek a job at a young age.

a. was forced b. necessitated c. has asked d. took

360. The ____________ boat was spotted off the shore.

a. lost b. missed c. escaped d. missing

361. _______ you not informed me, I wouldn't have known it.

a. If b. Unless c. Had d. Have

362. As he is ___________, he takes all the things seriously.

a. thin skinned b. thick skinned c. generous d. ignorant

363. The Prime Minister __________ the tricolour at the Red fort.

a. opened b. hoist c. inaugurated d. unfurled

364. Everybody is present today, ____________?

a. isn't it b. don't they c. aren't it d. aren't they

365. Every nook and ________ of the building was searched by the Police.

a. area b. corner c. top d. brook

366. He was taken to a / an ____________ destination last week.

a. closed b. unfortunate c. remoteful d. undisclosed

367. Inform me over phone once you __________ the hospital.

a. reach b. had reached c. reaches d. reached

368. The idea was ___________ by the present Chairman.

a. mooted b. raised c. opened d. nurtured

369. Alas ! His exit has been very much _____________.

a. hurt full b. indigesting c. inglorious d. upset

370. Don't speak in a _____________ way. Come to the point.

a. confusing b. cheating c. roundabout d.circuitful

371. Don't take ____________ 30 minutes to complete this task.

a. over b. more to c. beyond d. less than

372. The city witnessed ____________ security due to PM's visit.

a. overflow b. supreme

c. magnificent d. unprecedented

373. Turn off your computer now, otherwise it will be ________.

a. heated b. abnormal c. dangerous d. problematic

374. ____________ you completed the filing works till now ?

a. Haven't b. Aren't c. Didn't d. Weren't

375. Kindly wait here until the Manager __________ .

a. returns back b. returned c. appears d. returns

376. Suppose _________ you are rich . Will you help the poor ?

a. if b. imagine c. that d. none

377. The appropriate suffix for 'tutor' is ______________.

a. tutorial b. tutorship c. tutoring d. ial

378. Don't trust him as he is always _____________.

a. cheat b. dangerous c. trickster d. deceitful

379. The company gave us Rs. 5000/- for our _______ expenses.

a. sudden b. missing

c. miscellany d. miscellaneous

380. Regular __________ is very important for all activities.

a. practise b. practices c. practice d. practicing

381. ___________ that you reach the exam hall by 10 am.

a. Insure b. Surely c. Ensure d. Confer

382. After the meeting, we left ____ the hall at 3 pm.

a. over b. at c. from d. none

383. In case _____ you find any difficulty, call me immediately.

a. if b. when c. none d. that

384. Sundar's knowledge _________ English is stupendous.

a. over b. in c. on d. of

385. Madhu is extremely good ______ Mathematics.

a. in b. for c. at d. over

386. Everyone of them in the college ________ me very well.

a. know b. is knowing c. knows d. known

387. Only a quarter of the tank is full, ___________ ?

a. is it not b. doesn't it c. is it d. isn't it

388. Vinith has __________ revaluation for his Physics paper.

a. applying b. sent c. requested d. opted for

389. This patriot is one of the ________ sons of our village.
a. eldest b. oldest c. greater d. more

390. The ________ of the earthquake was really so devastating.
a. consequent b. impact c. results d. outcomes

391. He did not __________ the advice of his elders during his college days.
a. listen b. considered c. heed d. attention

392. __________ I go to my hometown, I visit that temple.
a. When ever b. Whenever c. Supposing d. Anytime

393. Avoid ________ talks to avoid misunderstanding.
a. loose b. lose c. carelessly d. unwanting

394. He is not an expert here ; he is merely a / an ________.
a. greenhorn b. average c. learning d. practicer

395. The office sent him several __________ regarding his leave.
a. remainders b. reminders
c. issues d. communications

396. The airport officials ______ the hidden documents.
a. sized b. seized c. confessed d. tore

397. Vimal is __________ to know his exam results these days.
a. eagerly b. curiously c. anxious d. worried

398. The adverb of the word, 'famous' is ___________.
a. fame b. familiarly c. famously d. famous

399. Nowadays __________ bookish knowledge is not enough.
a. merely b. mere c. few d. insufficient

400. ___________ the wild animal, he ran away at once.
a. Touching b. Seeing c. Heard d. Crossing

Answers

301. d	302. d	303. c	304. d	305. c
306. d	307. d	308. b	309. b	310. c
311. d	312. d	313. b	314. a	315. d
316. c	317. c	318. d	319. d	320. d
321. a	322. a	323. d	324. b	325. b
326. b	327. d	328. d	329. b	330. b
331. d	332. d	333. a	334. d	335. c
336. b	337. d	338. a	339. d	340. a
341. d	342. d	343. c	344. d	345. d
346. a	347. d	348. c	349. d	350. d
351. d	352. a	353. c	354. d	355. d
356. c	357. d	358. d	359. b	360. d
361. c	362. a	363. d	364. d	365. b
366. d	367. a	368. a	369. c	370. c
371. c	372. d	373. d	374. a	375. d
376. d	377. d	378. d	379. d	380. c
381. c	382. d	383. c	384. d	385. c
386. c	387. d	388. d	389. b	390. b
391. c	392. b	393. a	394. a	395. b
396. b	397. c	398. c	399. b	400. b

Your score now ____ /100

SECTION - E

Which of the following four is correct ?

401. He is ___________ of handling the sensitive matters.
a. uncapable b. inncapable c. unfit d. unused

402. He conceded just twelve runs in 7 overs. He is very _______.
a. economic b. economist c. economical d. loyal

403. In his __________ standard, he secured over 90 per cent.
a. eleven b. twelveth c. ten'th d. twelfth

404. " When did you see him _____ ?", the policeman asked me.
a. lastly b. lost c. last d. latest

405. We undertook the tour _______ the climate was very cold.
a. even b. nonetheless c. so d. inspite of

406. "Only a few of us __________ in rich families", he said.
a. have born b. born c. been born d. were born

407. Take three ___________ of milk to add with this.
a. three spoon b. three spoonfuls
c. three spoonsfuls d. three spoons

408. I saw a big black object ____________ in water.
a. drown b. sinks c. sinked d. sinking

409. It was a ______________ for him in the accident.
a. tragic b. close shave c. unfortunate d. escape

410. _____________ you go, take your ID card with you.
a. when ever b. where ever c. If need d. Wherever

411. The match was boring as the score __________ for long.
a. stationery b. was stationary
c. was stationery d. unmoving

412. Though Shyam and Bharath are friends, one can trust _____.
a. former b. the farmer c. the latter d. the later

413. "Never leave your job __________", the boss ordered.
a. un completed b. infinished
c. incompleted d. incomplete

414. "How long have ________ living here ?", she enquired me.
a. you b. been you c. your being d. you been

415. An optimist is one who finds __________ in every calamity.
a. hindrances b. opportunity c. problems d. solvation

416. "Once in a blue moon" means something that happens ___.
a. always b. never c. rarely d. repeatedly

417. Ramesh is innocent, but he has become a __________.
a. whitegoat b. red goat c. victimized d. scapegoat

418. The meaning of 'obliteration' is ____________.
a. destruction b. argument c. unhappy d. overpraise

419. Mohan is not ___________ as his brothers.
a. so stronger b. so wiser c. so taller d. so strong

420. "Priya has _______ seen the movie earlier", her sister said.
a. been b. to be c. yet to be d. not

421. They all came together for the ____________ held last week.
a. betroathal b. bedrothal c. betrothal d. new house

422. The ________ of this monument is it is made of a single rock.
a. unique b. uniqueness c. grateness d. salient

423. He is 'at sixes and sevens' means, he is in __________.
a. anger b. love c. sports d. confusion

424. The child played with the tiger cub _______ of the danger.
a. careless b. unmindedly
c. unmindfull d. unmindful

425. The truck driver applied sudden break to avoid the ______.
a. collusion b. collision c. collide d. clash

426. As Meena speaks ______________, everyone likes her.
a. occassionally b. rigidly
c. loudly d. candidly

427. The opposite of 'adventure' is ______.
a. unadventure b. misadventure
c. disadventure d. missadventure

428. The Director as well as the Secretary ____ sitting in the hall.
a. are being b. is been c. are d. is

429. Alas ! The injured ___________ in the hospital.
a. dead b. was died c. killed d. died

430. Don't repeat the same mistakes ___________.
a. again b. again and again
c. after d. none

431. Ultimately, Madhu ___________ her plans in public.
a. unclosed b. disclosed c. preclosed d. retold

432. I found ________ of the two books interesting.
a. all b. some c. neither d. first

433. A talkative boasting man is otherwise called ____________.
a. Big bag b. light bag c. ghost bag d. gasbag

434. The girls ___________ the boys in the terminal examination.
a. overscored b. outscored c. outcame d. out shined

435. The Manager ________ the unwanted sentences in the draft.
a. crosses b. overscored c. highlight d. shown

436. ___________ you apply now, it won't reach there tomorrow.
a. Otherwise b. If not c. Until d. Unless

437. Both the captains agreed to ______ the match due to bad light.

a. take off b. cancelled c. post pone d. call off

438. "If it is not__________, then whose one" ?, He said to me.

a. your's b. there's c. hers d. their's

439. "Your health needs a ________ check up", the doctor said.

a. regularly b. immediate c. properly d. thorough

440. The child laughs beautifully, ___________?

a. does it b. is it c. doesn't it d. isn't it

441. A new bridge has been constructed _________ the river.

a. over b. across c. into d. onto

442. Kindly _____ yourself from such hasty remarks.

a. distant b. away c. refrain d. avoid

443. If you want to live healthily, __________ from alcohol.

a. free b. remove c. relax d. abstain

444. Which letter is silent in the word, 'handsome' ?

a. m b. e c. o d. h

445. The word '___________' refers to something floating.

a. boyant b. buoyant c. drown d. fleet

446. Mohan has good ________ these days after his gym session.

a. physic b. physique c. shaped d. body

447. He has written several ________ articles during these years.

a. winning b. famously

c. award d. award-winning

448. Neither the chair nor the table _____ any scratches.

a. is b. have c. has d. are

449. Some of the _________ fans are in bad condition.

a. selling b. seiling c. ceiling d. sailing

450. Sangeetha is __________ than all in her family.

a. more happy b. happiest

c. happier d. more happier

451. I __________ he will attend the meeting tomorrow.

a. doubted b. don't think c. insure d. am doubted

452. He was ready with all his __________ for the one week tour.

a. paraphernalia b. luggages

c. thinks d. pockets

453. Unfortunately, __________ sank in the sea long ago.

a. the Ship b.The titans c. The Titanic d. The titanic's

454. Rohit wanted to __________ his studies abroad.

a. peruse b. pursue c. pursue for d. plan

455. Dinesh is __________ this type of climatic condition.

a. adopted b. accustomed with

c. accustomed to d. adapted to

456. The driver tried to __________ the curve to avoid accident.

a. overtake b. exceed c. avoid d. negotiate

457. The correct antonym of ' Member ' is __________.

a. demember b. dismember c. remember d. remover

458. Go there 'at once' means, " Go there __________".

a. only once b. immediately c. finally d. preparedly

459. " What a beautiful delivery" , is a / an __________ sentence.

a. Interrogative b. Informative

c. Exclamatory d. Imperative

460. The circus show __________ before the scheduled time.

a. was over b. has overed c. over d. has over

461. The traffic came to __________ during the Minister's visit.

a. standstill b. surprise c. crowded d. pathetical

462. The __________ for the rocket launching has started.

a. count down b. time

c. occasion d. countdown

463. The Manager's exit from the office has been ________.

a. untime b. inglorious c. sympathetic d. irregular

464. The __________ number is also called 'last but one'.

a. final b. penultimate

c. lowest d. approximate

465. There are countless __________ in all kinds of organisms.

a. spices b. speceies c. species d. varieties

466. Mentally _______ people are admitted in Lunatic asylum.

a. retorted b. retarted c. regarded d. retarded

467. __________! He has won the second round also.

a. Brave b. Kudos c. Supreme d. What

468. The _____ of the college was so good that I liked very much.

a. surroundings b. overview

c. ambience d. atmosphere

469. The word 'sesquicentennial' refers to a period of _______ years.

a. 175 b. 150 c. 300 d. 250

470. The _____________ for the state was excellently decorated.

a. tableax b. tabelax c. tableau d. tablex

471. __________ across the party line , everyone supported him.

a. all b. every c. Merely d. Cutting

472. " ______________ of the mangoes is ripened," she said.

a. Some b. Both c. Neither d. Few

473. A ___________ is also called a ' professional boxer'.

a. fighter b. wrestler c. puncher d. pugilist

474. Hema has been _______ her books to poor students for long.
    a. lent b. lends c. given d. lending
475. " Ignorance is a __________, isn't it ?", Swetha said.
    a. blessing b. pliss c. bliss d. waste
476. Nobody likes to live _____ that island, do they ?
    a. in b. to c. on d. with
477. Ashok is accustomed _______ live in such conditions.
    a. with b. by c. for d. to
478. Give him two ________ of the medicine after every meal.
    a. spoons b. spoonful c. spoonfuls d. spoonfull
479. This model is __________ unique in terms of the shape.
    a. real b. far c. mere d. none
480. The first and __________ chapter are really interesting.
    a. the last b. the second c. second d. the third
481. We got _________ to know about his untimely promotion.
    a. bewildered b. confused c. happy d. shock
482. Though this book is _________, it is highly informative.
    a. unexpensie b. costly c. inexpensive d. briefly
483. Rita asked me which of the two books I __________.
    a. have wanted b. want
    c. wanted d. will want
484. Don't force him to take a / an __________ decision now.
    a. instant b. decisive c. hasty d. quickly
485. Since time ____________, the library has served a lot.
    a. longer b. immemorial c. ago d. exists
486. The ___________ of the tiger was found near the hill.
    a. carcass b. dead body c. feetprint d. bones
487. __________ completes the task by today, will be rewarded.
    a. Who ever b. When she c. If they d. Whoever

488. A / An ____ is one who is an expert in curing child diseases.
a. Gynecologist b. Iconoclast
c. Physician d. Pediatrician

489. Don't ________ the words as it leads to confusion.
a. mis-pronunce b. unpronounce
c. un-utter d. mispronounce

490. The captain was given a __________ ovation after the match.
a. stand off b. excellent c. extraordinary d. standing

491. The PM was _______ a red carpet welcome at the airport.
a. shown b. taken c. gave d. accorded

492. The villagers took shelter under the roof for ________.
a. shading b. shadow c. safety d. escape

493. Why do they _____ this building even after the court order ?
a. occupying b. occupied c. occupy d. enjoy

494. Rajesh won the _________ by a whooping whisker.
a. match b. reward c. game d. sprint

495. Don't give _________ importance to petty things.
a. serious b. greatest c. undue d. high

496. To be happy in life, don't consider ________ matters.
a. tivial b.travial c. trivival d. trivial

497. The students ______ the science projects in the auditorium.
a. shown b. exercised c. exhibits d. demonstrated

498. Some of the school children suffered due to _____________.
a. dietary b. diets c. malnutrition d. hungry

499. Rewrite the following sentences ___________ direct speech.
a. making b. converting c. changing d. using

500. Which of the following is not a conjunction ?
a. That b. Unless c. weather d. If

Answers

401. b	402. c	403. d	404. c	405. b
406. d	407. b	408. d	409. b	410. d
411. b	412. c	413. d	414. d	415. b
416. c	417. d	418. a	419. d	420. d
421. c	422. b	423. d	424. d	425. b
426. d	427. b	428. d	429. d	430. d
431. b	432. c	433. d	434. b	435. b
436. d	437. d	438. c	439. d	440. c
441. b	442. c	443. d	444. b	445. b
446. b	447. d	448. c	449. c	450. c
451. b	452. a	453. c	454. b	455. c
456. d	457. b	458. b	459. c	460. a
461. a	462. d	463. b	464. b	465. c
466. d	467. b	468. c	469. b	470. c
471. d	472. c	473. d	474. d	475. c
476. c	477. d	478. c	479. d	480. c
481. a	482. b	483. c	484. c	485. b
486. a	487. d	488. d	489. d	490. d
491. d	492. c	493. c	494. d	495. c
496. d	497. d	498. c	499. d	500. c

Your score now ____ / 100

SECTION - F

Which of the following four is correct ?

501. Venkat's house is __________ the Indian bank, Tambaram.
a. opposite to b. over c. against d. opposite

502. __________ a few, all the teachers attended the meeting.
a. Indeed b. Barring c. Sparring d. With out

503. The word 'protagonist' refers to a ______________ character.
a. opposite b. formal c. super d. main

504. How old was he when he __________ the Indian Navy ?
a. occupied b. served c. released d. joined

505. Neither the story nor the character _______ uninteresting.
a. been b. are c. aren't d. is

506. It was not the driver's ______ that led to the accident.
a. careless b. oversight c. mistakes d. overdue

507. Akshaya ______________ responding to the questions.
a. has brilliantly b. has being
c. is being d. is brilliantly

508. The teacher said, " The satellite ____________ yesterday".
a. launched b. has launched
c. had launched d. was launched

509. ____________ is one who fights with the bull.
a. Patchman b. Batman c. Wrestler d. Matador

510. He 'fished in troubled waters' means, he won by ________.
a. hardly effort b. a big margin
c. practice d. unfair means

511. The road was closed by the PWD for the __________ works.

a. maintainance b. relying
c. maintenance d. official

512. Water supply has never __________ for the past three weeks.

a. stopped b. disrupted c. been disrupted d. ending

513. If one gets salary without doing any work, it is __________.

a. wasted b. mis-appropriate
c. sinecure d. illegal

514. Sundar's ________ to the post is quite appropriate.

a. occupation b. occupant c. occupancy d. occupied

515. I said to the bookseller, " Do you have __________ ?"

a. an other copy b. another copies
c. another copy d. more copy

516. The reindeer is a / an ____________, isn't it ?

a. quadrupped b. quadruped
c. element d. ecstatic

517. Mrs. Vidhya's __________ at the programme was excellent.

a. comparing b. compearing c. conducting d. compering

518. The speech delivered by the student was completely ______.

a. extemporic b. extemporeous
c. extempore d. imagination

519. The word similar to the word 'impromptu' is __________.

a. extempore b. magical c. prepared d. jovial

520. Only two of the failed students ________ removed from the roll.

a. is being b. have been c. has been d. are been

521. India almost won the match, ____________ ?

a. wasn't it b. didn't India c. isn't it d. didn't it ?

522. It was a / an __________ quiz solved by Ramya.

a. exceeding b. insurmountable

c. greatest d. toughest

523. 'Don't ________ the cat out of the bag', is an idiom.

a. throw b. keep c. open d. let

524. The idiom, ' break a leg' means __________.

a. accident b. bad luck c. run fast d. good luck

525. As the work was __________, I didn't go out.

a. incompleted b. uncomplete

c. incomplete d. not did

526. He will win when 'the pigs fly' means he will ________ win.

a. never b. sometimes c. surely d. at times

527. We have to do our works ourselves, __________?

a. don't we b. should we

c. can't we d. shouldn't we

528. Consult Mr. Gupta, a / an _____ in our area for eye diseases.

a. physician b. oculist c. physicist d. therapist

529. Albert Einstein was a renowned _____ during last century.

a. scientists b. physician c. physicist d. inventory

530. We checked all the __________ in our office thoroughly.

a. inventories b. bureau c. almirahs d. files

531. The President approved for the __________ of Parliament.

a. resolution b. desolation c. desolvation d. dissolution

532. The farmers expressed their ______ over the land issue.

a. languishes b. dissolution c. angry d. desolation

533. During Ashoka's _______, architecture flourished in India.

a. region b. time c. resume d. regime

534. 'Malady' is an old-fashioned word for __________.

a. decease b. ailment c. language d. Malaysia

535. The __________ are yet to be identified by the hospital.

a. diseased b. disease c. deaths d. deceased

536. '_______' words are no longer in use in our daily life.

a. cliché b. archice c. archaic d. Idiom

537. I fondly __________ my childhood days in my hometown.

a. remainder b. reminisce c. feeled d. longing

538. We use '__________ faithfully' while ending letters.

a. Your's b. Your c. Yours' d. Yours

539. His explanations are always __________________.

a. cell clear b. glass clear

c. crystally clear d. crystal clear

540. The word 'defunct' means, 'out of ____________'.

a. reach b. use c. purchase d. discussion

541. The __________ wedding of the deities was conducted with grandeur.

a. royal b. heavenly c. celestial d. ritual

542. Many students are __________ the results at present.

a. waiting b. waited c. awaited d. awaiting

543. You haven't submitted your files yet, ____________?

a. aren't you b. isn't it c. did you d. have you

544. All these properties __________ to our grandparents.

a. belonging b. belong

c. belongs d. are belonging

545. The factory gives ______ salary to all its employees.

a. luxuriously b. exorbitant c. highest d. handsome

546. It is one of the ___________ buildings in the heart of the city.

a. multy storied b. multistoried

c. multi storey d. multi-storyd

547. The house maid has kept all our things ___________.

a. intact b. in tact c. superbly d. domestically

548. The blood samples _______ sent to the laboratory recently.

a. will be b. is being c. has been d. have been

549. The police enquired about his _________ in a formal way.

a. historical b. proceedings

c. antisedents d. antecedents

550. All the departments _________ asked to submit the reports .

a. are been b. have been c. to have d. are to

551. The Indian hockey team is on the ___ of yet another victory.

a. blink b. threshold c. finally d. closure

552. The doctor advised me to take the tablets on _______ days.

a. alternatively b. every

c. alternate d. subsequence

553. He always ___________ independently in his office .

a. working b. was worked

c. worked d. work's

554. The meeting __________ as per the request of the members.

a. referred b. deferred

c. is being hold d. was deferred

555. The _________ body was cremated by the civic body.

a. discomposed b. decomposed

c. complete d. diffused

556. As the ___________ was not traced, the letter was returned.

a. addresse b. addressee c. sender d. receiver

557. This book _______ over 150 pages full of useful information.

a. consists b. comprises of

c. covers d. containing

558. Meena has been Priya's ___________ for many years.

a. confident b. friendly c. confidant d. bosom

559. This portrait is _________ than the other one on the wall.

a. more prettier b. more expensive

c. more costlier d. superior

560. A / An ___________ is for keeping arms and ammunition.

a. goodown b. deport c. arsenal d. dump yard

561. The word 'studious' means interested in ___________.

a. learning b. studios c. painting d. business

562. The young boy ___________ his father's burden.

a. lessoned b. lessened c. removed d. founded

563. Some of the universities were ___________ in 18th century.

a. found b. inaugurated c. notified d. founded

564. The '_____________' of this dish is quite interesting.

a. recipes b. ingredients c. taste d. recipe

565. If some one is on 'cloud nine', it means, he is ___________.

a. dead b. flying c. drunkard d. very happy

566. You can use my computer as long as it is __________.

a. error-free b. virus free c. worked d. necessity

567. As far as I __________, Ms. Jeyasri is a really good teacher.

a. concern b. known

c. agree d. am concerned

568. _________ you allow me to read this book for a while ?

a. If b. May c. Never d. Will

569. The reply given by the employee is ________________.

a. unsatisfied b. dissatisfied

c. unsatisfactory d. insatiable

570. Alas !He has become a ________ for the present scandal.

a. victimized b. nonsense c. scapegoat d. accused

571. The captain chose a / an _______ move just before the end.

a. unlawful b. favour

c. unprecedented d. indecent

572. He spoke just ordinarily. _________ he got the first prize.

a. Inspite b. So

c. As a result d. Nevertheless

573. Harish is ____________ to become a great entrepreneur.

a. learning b. yearning c. earning d. dwelling

574. She is my ______ cousin, Ms. Mathangi, who lives in Ooty.

a. own b. family

c. nearest d. brother-in-law's

575. India was bundled out for a _______ total of 78 runs.

a. poorly b. paultry c. pultry d. paltry

576. Exam results cannot be the only _______ to judge a student.

a. criteria b. method c. mean d. yardstick

577. As the dog was really __________ we were frightened.

a. humongous b. gorgeous c. rabies d. bitten

578. The _______ were crossing the road when the signal was on.

a. passengars b. pediatricians

c. pedestrians d. peoples

579. Writers use __________ language in prose, stories etc.,

a. prosaic b. unusual c. vague d. different

580. As compared to his brother, he is ___________, isn't he ?

a. latest b. more tall c. taller d. talksome

581. The term, ' fifth column' refers to secret or ________ groups.

a. lonely b. subversive c. rogues d. massive

582. It rained _________ in our city yesterday.

a. extremely b. cats and dogs
c. greatly d. largely

583. He was caught ___________ while accepting the bribe.

a. readily b. red handed c. proof d. nicely

584. I can't understand this. Kindly ___________ it for me.

a. simple b. paraphrase c. minimize d. read

585. Covid'19 seemed to be ____________ in all parts of globe.

a. commonly b. ubiquitous c. endangered d. existed

586. A board with the names of all faculties ________ in the hall.

a. were displayed b. was displayed
c. displayed d. shown

587. Your handwriting is ________________. Rewrite it now.

a. illegitimate b. illegal c. informal d. illegible

588. The city ___________ by the central government last week.

a. named b. renamed
c. was called d. was renamed

589. ___________ the success in the first movie, he started the second one.

a. Due b. Owing c. Following d. Because

590. The doctor asked him how his health ____________.

a. is now b. was now c. improved d. was

591. Neither postpone nor advance your work. Do it ________.

a. latter b. later c. well d. on time

592. The meeting remains _____ now due to hectic discussions.

a. unend b. inconclusive

c. uncompleting d. endlessly

593. Deepa, " It's half past three now, _________ ?"

a. isn't it b . it is c. No d. doesn't it

594. Who is the other ___________ of this document ?

a. signature b. signatore c. signator d. signatory

595. 'Stressfulness' is the ___________ form of 'stress'.

a. root b. suffix c. prefix d. etymology

596. As he has ______________, he hates women nowadays.

a. gynacs b. gynophobia c. gynoch d. hatred

597. Which of the following does the term ' of late ' refer to ?

a. belated b. past c. delayed d. recently

598. The ______________ customer left the shop angrily.

a. inpolite b. impatient c. curious d. irregular

599. Under ________ circumstances, we took a hasty decision.

a. unfirmly b. unruly c. unknown d. unforeseen

600. Due to ___________, he was debarred from the exam.

a. illegal b. inpersonation

c. mallpractice d. impersonation

Answers

501. d	502. b	503. d	504. d	505. d
506. b	507. d	508. d	509. d	510. d
511. c	512. c	513. c	514. c	515. c
516. b	517. d	518. c	519. a	520. b
521. d	522. b	523. d	524. d	525. c
526. a	527. d	528. b	529. c	530. a
531. d	532. d	533. d	534. b	535. d
536. c	537. b	538. d	539. d	540. b
541. c	542. d	543. d	544. b	545. d
546. c	547. a	548. d	549. d	550. b
551. b	552. c	553. c	554. d	555. b
556. b	557. a	558. c	559. b	560. c
561. a	562. b	563. d	564. d	565. d
566. b	567. d	568. d	569. c	570. c
571. c	572. d	573. b	574. d	575. d
576. d	577. a	578. c	579. a	580. c
581. b	582. b	583. b	584. b	585. b
586. b	587. d	588. d	589. c	590. d
591. d	592. b	593. a	594. d	595. b
596. b	597. d	598. b	599. d	600. d

Your score now ____ /100

SECTION - G

Which of the following four is correct ?

601. The word, 'jackdaw' refers to a kind of ______________.
a. equipment b. animal c. bird d. cheating

602. Nowadays Mr. Deepak lives __________ of this building.
a. in upstairs b. in upstair
c. upon the stairs d. upstairs

603. " These rooms are ___________", the inn keeper said to me.
a. changeable b. interchangeable
c. vacatable d. moderned

604. " Behave _______, otherwise, you will be charged", said he.
a. reasonable b. responsible
c. nobly d. responsibly

605. I had to console her as she was ______________.
a. foregone b. forlorn
c. forgotten d. forbearable

606. 'Pen is ____________ the sword', is a famous proverb.
a. greater than b. mighter than
c. superior to d. mightier than

607. The survey shows over 60 percent of the population ______
a. is graduate b. are graduate
c. graduated d. are graduates

608. Neither the drugs nor the dosages __________ him much.
a. helped to b. have helped
c. has helped d. did not help

609. Kindly post this letter this evening __________ from your office.

a. while returned b. while returning
c. after came d. when free

610. The Director cum Secretary of the Board __________ today.

a. has busy b. are busy
c. have been busy d. is busy

611. I suppose your behaviour is so __________ these days.

a. awe some b. disgraceful c. shabby d. unworthily

612. Where did ___________ your cell phone after charging ?

a. you left b. you kept c. you find d. you leave

613. An Iconoclast is one who is a ____________________.

a. reformer b. revolutionary
c. radical d. all these

614. The teacher told the class that the representative ________.

a. is ready b. is sincere
c. was sincere d. was arrogance

615. These advertisements are not only _______ but also bogus.

a. shameful b. misleading c. gorgeous d. genuine

616. __________ how hard he tries, he will never succeed.

a. No matter b. Despite c. Though d. Even if

617. If __________ alive, he would appear in a lot of movies.

a. he is b. he was c. he were d. he would

618. He helped me _________ the road when I was struggling.

a. to crossing b. cross c. to cross d. crossed

619. ______ the entire team, the captain held a press meet.

a. Represent b. Representing
c. On the behalf of d. Naming

620. " Keep all your _____ in your safe custody," the board read.

a. items b. jewelleries c. belonging d. valuables

621. Dr. Prem's family lives in the __________ of the city.

a. out skirt b. outskirts c. locality d. eastern

622. All of a sudden, a dark image ___________ in front of him.

a. appeared b. had appeared

c. was appeared d. raised

623. "Never be __________ in taking decisions", I advised him.

a. serious b. recklessly c. informal d. reckless

624. "It cannot be _________; it's mine," Rajeshwar said.

a. their's b. theirs c. your's d. our's

625. They built a memorial in the town to _______ his sacrifices.

a. publicize b. reward c. honour d. uproar

626. Don't try to change him, as he is ______________.

a. incorrectable b. unfair

c. incorrigible d. unfriendly

627. The opposite of int word,' incorrigible' is ____________.

a. redeemable b. refundable

c. impossible d. turncoat

628. A 'Turncoat' is a person who is a / an ___________.

a. betrayer b. defector c. traitor d. all these

629. The car fled the spot in a _____________ speed yesterday.

a. lightening b. lighting c. fastest d. lightning

630. The most important aspects of a subject is called, '_______'.

a. nitty gritty b. features

c. collectives d. memorabilia

631. The word 'souvenir' refers to a / an ___________.

a. option b. exercise c. priceless d. memento

632. Fear of being detached from cell phones is '________'.
a. nomophobia b. monophobia
c. Celtophobia d. acrophobia

633. __________ is an act of pretending to have moral values.
a. Hypocrite b. Biopsy c. Redeeming d. Hypocrisy

634. Looking at things in a shop without buying is called ______.
a. Cheating b. Fraudulent
c. Window shopping d. Pastime

635. We can make suffixes only with ____________.
a. verbs b. adjectives c. nouns d. all these

636. Abilash asked Vijay if ________ possibility of rain then.
a. there is b. there was c. it was any d. it might

637. The train _________ much before the passengers came.
a. arrived b. had left c. left d. has arrived

638. Vijay _______ the alarm to get up early in the morning.
a. set b. had put c. fixed d. adjusting

639. The ________ labourers left the site after the construction.
a. tiresome b. contract c. bonded d. poorest

640. We don't know why he took that decision ______ any logic.
a. unless b. without c. failing d. throwing

641. The idol was ____________ with diamond necklace.
a. put over b. put upon c. furnished d. bejeweled

642. ________ the villagers, the farmers also helped the victims.
a. Beside b. Apart c. Barring d. Besides

643. 'People _______ in glass houses, should not throw stones on others'.
a. residing b. who live c. who lived d. whose life

644. He was the __________ of the Fleet for our country.

a. Caption b. Admiral c. President d. Supreme

645. How long __________ living in New Delhi ?

a. are you b. were you

c. have you been d. are they

646. The team lost the match ____ its first innings lead of 128 runs.

a. though b. yet c. albeit d. shock to

647. President's Rule _______ in the state as per the notification.

a. replaced b. imposed

c. has been imposed d. at present

648. All the events of the Indian History have been ______ included.

a. decently b. alphabetically

c. actively d. chronologically

649. The idiom ' kicked the bucket' refers to __________.

a. anger b. death c. accident d. bribery

650. ________ novels are seldom read by the readers elsewhere.

a. Bogus b. Costliest c. Rarest d. Dreariest

651. It was a long ________ speech by the chief guest yesterday.

a. monologue b. monotonous

c. standing d. formal

652. The employees wanted their salaries ________ by the govt.

a. improved b. enlightened c. rised d. enhanced

653. Sangeetha is _______ her mother in many ways.

a. opposite to b. opposite c. opposite of d. resembled

654. Don't _______ your voice while speaking to your elders.

a. rose b. control c. raise d. downsize

655. The cabinet was _____ by the PM due to economic measures.

a. controlled b. removed c. exhausted d. downsized

656. One should cope _________ the stress at any cost.

a. up with b. with c. without d. within

657. The word ' columnist' refers to someone who is a/ an _____.

a. leader b. fighter c. journalist d. editor

658. A large number of visitors _______ to the museum today.

a. are come b. have come c. has come d. is coming

659. The word ' prelude' is a / an ___________ to a work.

a. summary b. paraphrase c. introduction d. ending

660. _______ is the culmination or ending of an event, work etc.,

a. Final b. Finalae c. Finale d. Prologue

661. Don't tell anything now as it is already ______________.

a. superfluous b. exaggerated c. unwanted d. maximum

662. Don't select him as he doesn't possess even ___ knowledge.

a. simple b. rudimentary c. superfluous d. subject

663. He is one of the ___________ of the Jaipur's royal family.

a. member b. decents

c. descendant's d. descendants

664. You could have collected the information ___________.

a. earliest b. before hand c. formerly d. beforehand

665. This is a really ___________ place to live in.

a. idol b. ideal c. formal d. fittest

666. 'Adam's apple' is found in human ______________.

a. stomach b. voice c. cerebrum d. throat

667. The audience couldn't hear the word as it was __________.

a. intolerable b. mispronounced

c. indirect d. noise

668. Though it was very expensive, it was ___________.
a. necessitated b. appraised
c. awesome d. obvious

669. 'Elegy' is a song related to _______________.
a. Devotion b. death c. friendship d. Love

670. Kindly ___________ the process, as it is already late.
a. expedite b. explore c. enquire d. ensure

671. The pilgrims felt ________ after the earthquake on the hill.
a. stranded b. problems c. lonely d. ashamed

672. This player is ___________ for the next match due to injury.
a. ruled out b. rules out
c. dropped into d. droped over

673. He answered all the tricky questions __________ .
a. satiable b. sagaciously c. fastly d. bravely

674. I feel your suffering as I am ___________.
a. emphatic b. sympathetic c. empathetic d. apathetic

675. Veena made such a / an __________ statement.
a. unique b. emphatic c. joyful d. suffering

676. As the property belongs to both of you, decide _________.
a. yourself b. yourselves' c. yourself's d. yourselves

677. The __________ is always smaller than that of an adult.
a. offshore b. outcome c. offspring d. lineage

678. The rebellions faced an utter __________ in the battle.
a. war b. uprising c. defeats d. fiasco

679. Some words in English are ________. Don't use them now.
a. indecent b. obsolete c. vulgar d. modern

680. Never use _______ words and phrases in communication.
a. discourteous b. dishonest
c. dizzy d. informal

681. If you feel ___________, consult your doctor.

a. dissatisfaction b. dizziness

c. disaster d. dragging

682. It was a / an ___________ in the auditorium last night.

a. imbroglio b. rowdyism c. comedy d. fiasco

683. Some ________ in the mob pelted stones on the vehicles .

a. illegals b. bachelors c. miscreants d. pedestrians

684. Prem has been a ___________ of God since his college days.

a. theist b. disbeliever c. responder d. atheist

685. A / An __________ thinks people do good for their own.

a. lyricist b. cynic c. florist d. oculist

686. The passengers were _______ when the pilot was speaking.

a. listened b. listened to c. listening d. all ears

687. "_________" means using the mightiest power ever before.

a. On all cylinders b. Dashing

c. Bombastic d. Hazzling

688. The word' 'penury' is closely related to __________.

a. disease b. poverty c. economy d. suffering

689. _____ have same spelling, but meanings and pronunciation differ.

a. Homophone b. Homogenes

c. Hmophs d. Homographs

690. The word' Resume' is an example for ______________.

a. Homograph b. Homophone

c. Homonym d. Writing

691. 'Although he spoke well he wasn't encouraged' is a ____ sentence.

a. simple b. complex c. compound d. peculiar

692. The rains are ____________ in our town even now.

a. stopped b. raining c. inundated d. increasing

693. This painting is ________ unique in the Centenary Hall.

a. beautifully b. more c. most d. none

694. It was a __________ fantastic shot by Sachin Tendulkar.

a. most b. very c. more d. none

695. Cricket is a game of __________ as known to everyone.

a. capriciousness b. turns

c. shocks d. successes

696. The prisoners were ________ by the escorting policeman.

a. handcuffed b. handcuffled

c. handled d. caught

697. The BCCI announced the new ____________ for the tour.

a. initiative b. itinerary

c. scheme d. administration

698. Don't believe him ; he sheds __________ tears.

a. unnatural b. falsely c. fake d. crocodile

699. Your words are confusing. Make then __________.

a. understand b. specially c. logic d. crystal clear

700. We __________ knew when he left Tokyo for the new job.

a. didn't b. never c. cannot d. always

Answers

601. c 602. d 603. b 604. d 605. b
606. d 607. d 608. b 609. b 610. d
611. b 612. d 613. d 614. c 615. b
616. a 617. c 618. b 619. b 620. d
621. b 622. a 623. d 624. b 625. c
626. c 627. a 628. d 629. d 630. a
631. d 632. a 633. d 634. c 635. d
636. b 637. b 638. a 639. b 640. b
641. d 642. d 643. b 644. b 645. c
646. c 647. c 648. d 649. b 650. d
651. b 652. d 653. c 654. c 655. d
656. b 657. c 658. b 659. c 660. c
661. a 662. b 663. d 664. d 665. b
666. d 667. b 668. a 669. b 670. a
671. a 672. a 673. b 674. c 675. b
676. d 677. c 678. d 679. b 680. a
681. b 682. a 683. c 684. b 685. b
686. d 687. a 688. b 689. d 690. a
691. b 692. c 693. d 694. d 695. a
696. a 697. b 698. d 699. d 700. b

Your score now ___/100

SECTION - H

Which of the following four is correct ?

701. The building seems to be __________ as it's centuries old.
a. ancient b. dilapidated c. cracking d. taller

702. The Board decided to _______ the building as its condition is bad.
a. Destroy b. downgrade
c. pull down d. remove

703. The word' 'Kindness' is a / an ____________ noun.
a. collective b. common c. abstract d. simple

704. Wait ________ the water boils to its optimum level.
a. for b. untill c. unless d. until

705. Nowadays , reading books is not just my __________ .
a. hobbies b. pastime c. profession d. likening

706. Why do you want to ______ documents photocopied now ?
a. see the b. make the c. get the d. taking the

707. Many students are trained on the matters of _______ skills.
a. laborious b. organizational
c. fundamental d. possessive

708. The word 'tightfisted' refers to the ________ attitude of a person.
a. powerful b. selfish c. innocent d. fighting

709. The prisoner was taken to a / an ____________ location.
a. remotest b. unspecific
c. inconclusive d. undisclosed

710. The netting board on which one can bounce anyways is ________.

a. Trampoline b. Tripoline

c. fastrope d. netjump

711. Which of the following is related to battle, argument, clash etc., ?

a. face lift b. face off c. face out d. face over

712. The word' facelift' means an operation to ____________.

a. remove teeth b. remove nose

c. look younger d. change eyes

713. What do you mean by 'Wuthering ' ?

a. Destroying b. Windy c. Concluding d. Drying

714. If something is noisy or showy or ostentatious, it is ________.

a. exorbitant b. excessive c. flamboyant d. superb

715. A / An ________ is someone who pretends to be another.

a. Fraudstor b. Cheat c. Imposter d. Queer

716. At least two of us ________ Queen's English these days.

a. are knowing b. can speak

c. speaks d. knows

717. Remember that you are ____________ winning the contest.

a. capable to b. capable of

c. definite for d. entitled to

718. Don't travel in 2nd class when you are ________ AC II Tier.

a. allowed to b. right to

c. used to d. entitled for

719. In the event of ________ the course, we will pay the fees.

a. you join b. your join

c. your joined d. your joining

720. The __________ boy always came late to the classes.

a. stupidly b. uneagerly c. sluggish d. challenging

721. 'The _________ catches the pray' is an interesting proverb.

a. active bird b. hungry lion c. first animal d. early bird

722. Never argue with a / an _______, as it leads to chaos.

a. liars b. foe c. dunce d. foolish

723. He consulted a Neurologist as he had prolonged _______.

a. pains b. diseases c. fallings d. dizziness

724. " You _________ post your letter which is always better."

a. should b. can c. always d. yourself

725. They finished all the work just in a / an ____________.

a. surprise b. fraction c. overnight d. fourtnight

726. It is a really _________ monument, isn't it ?

a. glorified b. greatest c. picturesque d. historical

727. This judge has delivered a ___________ verdict recently.

a. historical b. superlative c. maximum d .historic

728. After the flood _______, resume your construction works.

a. completes b. resumes c. completed d. receded

729. These books are obviously __________ the other books.

a. costly than b. costlier to c. costlier than d. worst than

730. The Parliament gave ____ to the Bill despite the opposition.

a. ok b. knot c. nod d. signalling

731. _______ tomorrow, kindly meet me on Friday next.

a. Inspite of b. Instead of c. Besides d. As far

732. "If winter comes, can _______ be far behind" ? is a fabulous quote.

a. summer b. autumn c. spring d. rains

733. He has scored more than fifteen centuries ______________.

a. in abroad   b. outside   c. in debut   d. overseas

734. As my sister is working ________, I feel as lonely as a hill.

a. abroad   b. foreign   c. for away   d. in MNC

735. The employees were informed ___________ about this.

a. earliest   b. all ready

c. surely   d. beforehand

736. ___________ a chance, I would select the second option.

a. Giving   b. To give   c. Given   d. Taking

737. The word' 'intramural' refers to _________ the institution.

a. besides   b. within   c. away from   d. denote

738. The massive _____ of the visitors has boosted the economy.

a. reporting   b. arrive   c. influx   d. exit

739. The antonym of the word ' gratitude " is _______________.

a. ungratitude   b. disgratitude

c. ingratitude   d. misgratitude

740. The prefix ' infra' gives the meaning _______________.

a. highest   b. below   c. excessive   d. invisible

741. The usage RSVP means ' ___________ silvous plait'

a. Respondez   b. Respond   c. Receipt   d. receive

742. A mistake in the use of language is ___________.

a. solvism   b. solecism   c. insolvent   d. slip

743. Nowadays he __________ drive the car himself.

a. used to   b. could   c. can   d. may

744. "When _________ movie screened here ?", I said to him.

a. did the last   b. the last   c. was the last   d. the latest

745. ________ was unprepared for the interview, he skipped it.

a. Though he   b. As it   c. Since his   d. As he

746. Ankit can write with both hands, as he is __________.

a. ambiguous b. ambidextrous
c. outstanding d. eccentric

747. "Don't use ________ to win the match,", the referee warned.

a. illegal terms b. bogus points
c. tricks d. unfair means

748. I want to __________ my bad habits at any cost.

a. clear over b. cross over c. get rid off d. get rid of

749. This is a wonderful park for children's ________.

a. hobby b. nature
c. entertain d. amusement

750. The PM ________ the new train service from the capital.

a. established b. resumed c. flags of d. flagged off

751. The system of naming things, especially in science is _____.

a. huriculture b. jeoculture
c. nomenculture d. nomenclature

752. He would never do anything to ________ his career.

a. endanger b. spoilt c. jeopardize d. waste

753. The antonym of the word 'jeopardize' is __________.

a. careless b. protection c. safeguard d. retaliate

754. The India _______ England match has ended in a draw.

a. verses b. against c. opposing d. versus

755. We stood _________ at the site of the accident.

a. lonely b. aghast c. terrible d. ruthless

756. The collector promised to __________ the civic works.

a. execute b. evacuate c. entrust d. accelerate

757. 'There is many a slip _____ the cup and the lip' is a proverb.

a. beyond b. before c. with d. twixt

758. 'Don't count your chickens before ____________.'

a. they form b. they come c. it comes d. they hatch

759. A kind of precaution to stop an action is ' to __________ '.

a. neglect b. preempt c. foresee d. yield

760. " Action ___________ louder than words'. So, act at once.

a. is b. speaks c. speak d. sounds

761. ____________ fascinating all these stories are !

a. What a b. How c. How many d. Alas

762. It's extremely difficult to ___________ between the two .

a. combine b. compere c. identify d. differentiate

763. As we are busy now, please meet us on _________ occasion.

a. alternate b. another c. following d. various

764. " _______ is found guilty, will be punished," the boss said.

a. whomover b. whoever c. who ever d. wherever

765. Don't be in a hurry, as we are ___________________.

a. ahead time b. more time

c. lot of time d. ahead of time

766. You are answerable only to the Manager, not ________ else.

a. anyone b. any one c. every one d. someone

767. I walked freely as I didn't know the meaning of '________'.

a. No walking b. Not allowed

c. No crossing d. No thoroughfare

768. Which of the following is not a punctuation mark ?

a. parenthesis b. colon

c. pause d. period

769. Elephants are sent to __________ centres periodically.

a. animal b. reserved

c. activating d. rejuvenating

770. We are on __________ to know the results.

a. obvious b. tenterhooks
c. afraid d. anxious

771. __________ all the students are wearing ID cards today.

a. Luckily b. Usually
c. Unknowingly d. Surprisingly

772. The cellphone was kept ________ the two cots.

a. over b. betwixt c. under d. besides

773. Only 2 percent of the population ______ the local language.

a. are knowing b. know's
c. have known d. don't know

774. "Hobson's choice' means almost __________ .

a. no choice b. everywhere c. nowhere d. everyone

775. The young woman was attacked for a/ an _______ money.

a. meagre b. break c. rich d. decent

776. The ruling party won the election with a / an __________ majority.

a. thumping b. superbly
c. whoop d. accumulating

777. "Better ________ ; than rust out". So work hard.

a. wear out b. burn out c. throw out d. lay out

778. As his behavious was ________ , the police followed him.

a. doubting b. mysterious c. suspicious d. doubtfull

779. It ________ , not his brother who won the prize twice.

a. was he b. is him c. is his d. was whom

780. The Republic day __________ was so gorgeous this year.

a. parades b. tableau c. tricolours d. security

781. Why __________ you sit with her as she feels lonely ?

a. won't b. can not c. don't d. did

782. The leader is on a hunger strike from ____________.

a. dawn to dusk b. morning

c. now to then d. Monday

783. In the event of __________, we are likely to appoint him.

a. his acceptance b. he accepting

c. his joining d. clearance

784. George Bernard Shaw was a _______________ .

a. teatotaller b. teetotallar c. poorer eater d. teetotaller

785. The collector _______ the media of the flood situation.

a. informed b. apprise c. apprised d. appraised

786. Nothing can shake you ________ you are mentally strong.

a. otherwise b. Untill c. if d. unless

787. Kindly avoid __________ language, as it hurts people.

a. misuse b. offensive c. unpolitely d. precarious

788. During summer ____________ , people run short of water.

a. season b. times c. duration d. none

789. Children prefer __________ snacks to fruit salads.

a. sugar b. tasted c. sugary d. sugarly

790. He _______ my suggestion that we should change the date.

a. welcome b. agreed with c. agreed to d. denied

791. My friend got _________ when he got too many options.

a. confessed b. bewildered

c. confuse d. embarrassing

792. Which one of the following means ' brother' or 'sister' ?

a. cousins' b. sibling c. sons d. daughters

793. Raji is not only my cousin ________ but also a well wisher.

a. sister b. friend c. relative d. none

794. Writers use ________ to evoke feelings among the readers.

a. irony b. pathos c. climax d. sympathy

795. The words 'lift' and 'elevator' are examples of __________.

a. antonym b. heteronym c. simile d. meanings

796. A person whose career is more important than anything else is ________.

a. careerism b. careerist c. captivist d. columnist

797. Please ________ understand the importance of the transfer.

a. tell him b. make him c. make to him d. brief to him

798. In case ______ you have signed the copy, you can go now.

a. if b. do c. did d. none

799. The Principal ______ the staff to cooperate with the system.

a. wished b. appealed to c. told to d. arose

800. Among the 50 students, only ______ have not brought the book.

a. one b. few c. a few d. somebody

Answers

701. b	702. c	703. c	704. d	705. b
706. c	707. b	708. b	709. d	710. a
711. b	712. c	713. b	714. c	715. c
716. b	717. b	718. d	719. d	720. c
721. d	722. c	723. d	724. a	725. c
726. d	727. d	728. d	729. c	730. c
731. b	732. c	733. d	734. a	735. d
736. c	737. b	738. c	739. c	740. b
741. a	742. b	743. c	744. c	745. d
746. b	747. d	748. d	749. d	750. d
751. d	752. c	753. c	754. d	755. b
756. d	757. d	758. d	759. b	760. b
761. b	762. d	763. b	764. b	765. d
766. a	767. d	768. c	769. d	770. b
771. d	772. b	773. d	774. a	775. a
776. a	777. a	778. c	779. a	780. b
781. c	782. a	783. a	784. d	785. c
786. c	787. b	788. d	789. c	790. c
791. b	792. b	793. d	794. b	795. b
796. b	797. b	798. d	799. b	800. c

Your score now /100

SECTION - I

Which of the following four is correct ?

801. We knew the results already. It's merely ______________.
a. formality b. reality
c. fait accompli d. boring

802. Eating with spoons is their __________ manners.
a. familiar b. familial c. tradition d. modern

803. You are a liar and I don't want to hear anymore _________.
a. comics b. fairytales c. rubbish d. stories

804. Some of the crimes come under '_________' category.
a. vigilant b. punishable
c. zero tolerance d. in evitable

805. The ability to express oneself well is called '_________'.
a. oration b. oracle c. oracy d. strength

806. A person who behaves unusually and independently is a ____.
a. unique b. eccentricity c. peculiar d. maverick

807. It is his ______ that he desires for more power, wealth etc.,
a. stupidity b. greedy c. cupidity d. luck

808. We _________ him from the club due to his ill manners.
a. resigned b. dismembered
c. thrown d. vacated

809. Everyone of the committee ____ aware of the development.
a. are b. has c. have been d. is

810. Neither of his two sons ___________ at the funeral.
a. presented b. was present c. was appeared d. were

811. I am in a hurry. Kindly ________ the important points.
a. intimate to b. inform of c. not down d. jot down

812. The Japanese art of folding papers for decorations is _____.
a. Twingo b.. martial c. origami d. shwepeye

813. Though he is a / an __________ singer, his voice is good.
a. rarest b. occasional c. formal d. renowned

814. My quest for learning English is ____________.
a. unreachable b. unfortunate
c. unquenchable d. manageable

815. Something that serves as a measure for others is ________.
a. model b. benchmark c. potential d. follower

816. Don't believe in __________ as it may be false or baseless.
a. haresay b. hearsay c. rumours d. lies

817. Quite a few members of the committee ____ in the meeting.
a. presenting b. presented
c. are presented d. are present

818. _______ a little cautious you could have saved yourself.
a. if you were b. Had you be
c. Were you d. Had you been

819. Everyone knows that Ooty is __________ Kodaikkanal.
a. cold as b. colder than c. more cold d. colder to

820. The _________ reforms are being carried out gradually.
a. economic b. economical c. modern d. world's

821. Ajay never interfered with your personal matters, ______?
a. didn't he b. did he c. isn't it d. wasn't he

822. You will open a new account tomorrow, ___________?
a. is it b. is it not c. will you d. won't you

823. Some books __________ translated into English recently.
a. are being b. has been c. have been d. are been

824. Let's not discuss ________ the matter now, as it is trivial.
a. on b. about c. with the d. none

825. The building __________ vacant for at least three months.

a. is being b. has been

c. has being d. should not been

826. As he had a __________, he seemed to be dull.

a. running nose b. feverish

c. problem d. runny nose

827. __________ waiting for the train, I met my friend.

a. During b. While c. Whenever d. Suddenly

828. __________ appeared before me all of a sudden.

a. Mine friend b. A friend of my

c. A my friend d. A friend of mine

829. The bank is at __________ distance from my house.

a. a walkable b. walking c. some d. nearest

830. She accepted the company's proposal __________.

a. wishingly b. willy-nilly

c. nearly d. regularly

831. We __________ a cup of tea at the restaurant.

a. cancell b. ordered

c. may ordering d. drunk

832. The baby was __________ Pinky at a function in Mumbai.

a. named as b. named

c. called as d. named after

833. The Memorial was __________ Dr. A.P.J. Abdul Kalaam.

a. named b. named as c. named after d. called

834. The bank wants to __________ the post of a Manager.

a. fill in b. fulfil c. appoints d. complete

835. He is sincere. __________, I don't trust him.

a. Even though b. Even so

c. Despite d. Even

836. The best teacher was ___________ a cash prize.

a. awarded b. awarded with

c. awarded for d. honoured

837. This hall is ______________ to conduct the examination.

a. sufficient enough b. sufficient

c. meant for d. not

838. ___________ was wasted in the meeting this morning.

a. An whole hour b. A whole hour

c. A hour d. The hour

839. The phrase 'null and void' means _____________.

a. not because b. no legal bearing

c. acceptable d. untrue

840. The court declared the by election '_____________'.

a. conduct b. cancelling c. null and void d. violence

841. The protocol was to some extent ________ by the institution.

a. adapted b. breached c. neglected d. reached

842. He ___________ in a robbery case last year.

a. accused of b. accused off

c. was accused d. was accused of

843. The umpire awarded 'No ball' as the bowler _____________.

a. is overstep b. is overstepping

c. over stepped d. overstepped

844. The revised schedule _________ announced soon by BCCI.

a. is being b. will to be c. will be d. will being

845. Don't think he is not listening. He is '_____________'.

a. acting b. all years c. clever d. all ears

846. The idiom 'Close shave' means ______________.

a. miserly b. ridiculously

c. narrow escape d. nearing

847. The study of the origin and history of words is '________'.
a. word power b. syllable c. phonetics d. etymology

848. ________ is the study of coins, medals etc.,
a. Forensics b. Numismatics c. Acoustics d. Semantics

849. The branch of linguistics concerning with meaning is '____'.
a. Etymology b. Semantics c. Originology d. Fun search

850. ________ is a person who knows a lot about art, music etc.,
a. Literattter b. Connoisseur c. Litterateur d. Wizard

851. Which of the following doesn't have 'mis' as its prefix ?
a. fortune b. match c. happening d. universe

852. Padma is always __________ in her conversation.
a. candidly b. outspoken c. softly d. honest

853. The first design from which other copies are made is _____.
a. priotype b. phototype c. prototype d. sterotype

854. Which of the following is not a primary colour ?
a. Red b. Yellow c. Blue d. Green

855. The word ' pie-eyed' refers to a person who is __________.
a. blind b. unlucky c. dying d. overdrunk

856. A 'phrasal verb' is a combination of a verb and a/ an _____.
a. preposition b. adverb
c. both a and b d. auxiliary verb

857. My mother cooks deliciously. Here ' deliciously' is a / an ____.
a. preposition b. adjective c. phrase d. adverb

858. Do you think that the hotel will ________ tomorrow ?
a. opens b. be open c. continue d. inaugurate

859. Be __________ for the inspection to be held tomorrow.
a. prepare b. curious c. anxious d. prepared

860. Very few states in India are ________ Sikkim.
a. smaller to b. as small as c. farther than d. tinier than

861. Why did you_______ for the eleventh hour to complete it ?
a. wait for b. wait c. assume d. delay

862. The __________ students were warned not to repeat it.
a. mistaked b. errous c. erring d. faulty

863. We made a _____________ request to the Principal.
a. small b. begin c. benign d. strong

864. The journalist asked the politician __________ politics.
a. when entered b. how he entered
c. why entered d. what is

865. __________ deals with ' Subject- verb agreement' .
a. grammar b. tense c. concord d. vocabulary

866. ________ is used in the phrase ' the deafening silence.'
a. simile b. metaphor c. hyperbole d. oxymoron

867. "Be as cool as cucumber" . The figure of speech used is ___.
a. climax b. antithesis c. simile d. metaphor

868. Don't spend your money _________ before the tour starts.
a. foolishly b. wastely c. sufficiently d. lavishly

869. He was so ______ that he praised his opponent's win.
a. magnificent b. greater c. gracious d. graciously

870. As he knew none of the answers, he wrote ___________ .
a. blank b. anything c. nothing d. sincerely

871. She wanted to know why we _________ our home work.
a. had not b. had not done
c. missed d. failed

872. During the vacation I really enjoyed ___________.
a. myself b. as much c. greatly d. none

873. Ajay has returned ________ from the foreign trip recently.
a. back b. soon c. quickly d. none

874. "Could you __________ me cross the road now ?" he said.

a. help b. help out c. help to d. have helped

875. There is no ___________ to anyone from the rule.

a. excuse b. exemption c. escape d. relax

876. Don't underestimate him ; he is a __________ in his field.

a. past master b. magnet c. newcomer d. diamond

877. Sudha's __________ at the party was really gorgeous.

a. gait b. galore c. galaxy d. absence

878. We experienced _________ rains during last week.

a. heaviest b. copious c. floppy d. rigorous

879. Everyone is watching the show, ___________ ?

a. isn't it b. isn't he c. aren't they d. is it not

880. I am looking after the department, ___________ ?

a. aren't I b. am I c. isn't it d. am not

881. Aren't you aware that we need a __________ room ?

a. greater b. bigger c. longest d. uniform

882. Revise the chapter _____ two days as the exam is nearing.

a. until b. with in c. for d. within

883. The ______ view was so beautiful that it attracted everyone.

a. geographic b. panoramic c. bird's d. rapid

884. A / an _________ statue of the poet was unveiled yesterday.

a. overall b. life-size c. portrait d. half top

885. It _________ that only a few had not paid fees.

a. was observe b. was notice

c. could see d. was noticed

886. Many ____________ in the fire accident yesterday.

a. were died b. were dead

c. more dead d. were feared dead

887. The students had a / an____________ enjoyment.
a. euphoric b. interested c. all round d. powerful

888. The hoarding was fixed _______ the tall building.
a. over b. atop c. into d. besides

889. Newspapers offer concessional charges for ______ columns.
a. dying b. death c. obituary d. educative

890. Your sister has not seen this house, _____________?
a. doesn't she b. has she c. hasn't she d. wasn't she

891. Don't be ___________ with your present status.
a. proud b. competent c. complacent d. settle

892. Nothing is impossible for a / an ____________ student.
a. beautiful b. young c. excellently d. industrious

893. __________ the bus was overcrowded, I didn't travel on it.
a. Perhaps b. As c. Though d. Due to

894. ___________ was the construction carried out ?
a. Who b. Whom c. By whom d. Whose

895. __________ take a good decision on his own.
a. Let him b. Let we c. Let his d. He need to

896. All the roads __________ to the airport are sealed by police.
a. leads b. that leads c. going d. leading

897. Mercury is __________ of all the metals.
a. strongest b. the heaviest c. the biggest d. thickest

898. How long __________ waiting for us, dear friends ?
a. are you b. have you
c. have been d. have you been

899. He __________ the midnight oil to succeed in the exam.
a. burnt b. used c. wasted d. allowed

900. Umpires/ Referees are always _______ on and off the field.
a. unattached b. unbiassed c. unnatural d. unruly

Answers

801. c	802. b	803. b	804. c	805. c
806. d	807. c	808. b	809. d	810. b
811. d	812. c	813. b	814. c	815. b
816. b	817. d	818. d	819. b	820. a
821. b	822. d	823. c	824. d	825. b
826. d	827. b	828. d	829. b	830. b
831. b	832. b	833. c	834. a	835. b
836. a	837. b	838. b	839. b	840. c
841. b	842. d	843. d	844. c	845. d
846. c	847. d	848. b	849. b	850. b
851. d	852. b	853. c	854. d	855. d
856. c	857. d	858. b	859. d	860. b
861. b	862. c	863. c	864. b	865. c
866. d	867. c	868. d	869. c	870. c
871. b	872. a	873. d	874. a	875. b
876. a	877. a	878. b	879. c	880. a
881. b	882. d	883. b	884. b	885. d
886. d	887. a	888. b	889. c	890. b
891. c	892. d	893. b	894. c	895. a
896. d	897. b	898. d	899. a	900. b

Your score now ___/100

SECTION - J

Read the following and spot the error.

If there is no error, mark "D"

901. One has to wait (A) and watch till the (B) final results is announced. (C)
902. The ingredients of this (A) dish is (B) easily available everywhere. (C)
903. Kindly conform that (A) such things do not (B) occur again in future. (C)
904. Everyone adhere (A) to the rules and regulations (B) of the institution. (C)
905. Since his was (A) highly educated he (B) doesn't believe in superstitions. (C)
906. "Where have you (A) been all these days?"(B), I said toward him. (C)
907. The woman standing (A) here is (B) Prem's and Manu's mother. (C)
908. Inspite of his (A) repeated successes (B), he remains humble always. (C)
909. The tourists were (A) enroute to their hometown (B) after visiting the sites. (C)
910. I will never remember (A) your timely help that (B) led to my successful career. (C)

911. In the event of your (A) reaching the airport firstly, (B) kindly inform me. (C)

912. The publisher said, (A) "This book comprises of (B) nearly two hundred pages." (C)

913. The distance between (A) the bank and my college (B) are just 3 kms. (C)

914. As Shyam is a erudite (A) person, he knows how (B) to handle this. (C)

915. If you had (A) told me in advance (B) I would have been alerted myself. (C)

916. Dhivya congratulated (A) me over phone (B) on mine's promotion. (C)

917. As these are rotten (A) apples, I request you to (B) keep it aside now. (C)

918. We have celebrated (A) the Martyr's Day (B) on our campus quite recently. ©

919. "Be quite !", my mother said." The child is sleeping (B). Don't disturb it." (C)

920. Everyone knows (A) that Meena resembles (B) like her elder sister, Karthika. (C)

921. Nithya speaks Hindi (A) occasionally and rarely, (B) but very much fluently. (C)

922. Unmindful to (A) the consequences, he entered into (B) an argument with his friend. (C)

923. "Can you be able (A) to attend today's online (B) classes without fail?", (C)

924. Putting his cellphone (A) in his hands, he was (B) searching for it everywhere.(C)

925. I made a huge loss (A) by accepting the project(B) which was really new to me. (C)

926. A very purpose (A) of my coming here is (B) to meet some of my old friends. (C)

927. Can I submit (A) the assignment some time (B) in the evening today,?" I said. (C)

928. Though he comes (A) to the class lately, (B) he is quite attentive and brilliant. (C)

929. Having lost (A) my passport, I applied (B) for a new passport. (C)

930. I will not buy (A) any apple as its purchase has (B) given me bitter experience. (C)

931. The time when (A) the flight departs (B) are not known to anyone. (C)

932. Nobody is knowing (A) how these incidents (B) have come about.(C)

933. Why do the office (A) allow payments to be (B) made in currencies ? (C)

934. The use of alcohol (A) and narcotics is an (B) open invitation to death. (C)

935. Owing to ill health (A) the Minister was resigned (B) from the post. (C)

936. Unless you start now,(A) you will be able not (B) to reach the airport on time. (C)

937. Don't tell your (A) cock and bull story, (B) as I know the entire truth. (C)

938. Though he put the (A) alarm for 6 am, (B) he could get up only at 7 am.(C)

939. If you cannot (A) respect your profession, (B) better you have quit it. (C)

940. As the delivery of the (A) goods got inordinate delay, (B) I cancelled the order.(C)

941. 'The pen is mightier than (A) the sword' is a (B) well known popular statement. (C)

942. As they are (A) mentally matured, (B) they will take care of themself. (C)

943. "Don't repeat the (A) same mistakes again and again.", (B) the Manager said. (C)

944. As the train was arrived (A) late by ten minutes, (B) we were lucky to catch it. (C)

945. "Never ride your bike (A) on the wronger side", (B) the policeman warned me. (C)

946. Is it not our duty (A) to cope up with (B) the present difficult situation ? (C)

947. Our food habits (A) place a vital role (B) in maintaining our health. (C)
948. Due to extremely poverty, (A) he had to meet (B) with this unfortunate end.(C)
949. If you want progress, (A) try to give in (B) your bad habits at once. (C)
950. One of the exercises (A) in this book are (B) meant for children's activities. (C)
951. Mahesh used to (A) draw pencil sketches during childhood , (B) wasn't he ? (C)
952. The exodus of foreigners (A) has really boosted (B) the economy of the city. (C)
953. 'All that glitters is (A) not a gold' is a well known (B) proverb , isn't it ?. (C)
954. The book as well as its (A) contents are very useful (B) to all the learners, (C)
955. Lalitha is all ears (A) when she attends (B) any online programme. (C)
956. You may perhaps (A) have to read the passage (B) twice to understand. (C)
957. The child to be (A) taught how to count numbers (B) using simple techniques.(C)
958. I don't think he is (A) capable of writing essays (B) in English without mistakes.(C)

959. It is very common to (A) see people walking barefoot (B) due to faith in God. (C)

960. The story is not so (A) interested as you had (B) told me a few days ago. (C)

961. Nobody was not even (A) able to hear the voice (B) as it was so feeble. (C)

962. Out of the nine times (A) that he contested, (B) he could won only twice.(C)

963. The actor asked his (A) fan to get his autograph (B) at some other occasion. (C)

964. Don't spend money (A) on unnecessary things, (B) as it is a white elephant. (C)

965. Many of his friends (A) attended his birthday party (B) ever without invitation. (C)

966. I can't immediately (A) grand you permission. (B) Give me sometime to think.(C)

967. As soon as the chief guest (A) arrived, everyone had (B) greeted him warmly. (C)

968. The word,' simultaneous' (A) an adverb, means (B)' happening at the same time'. (C)

969. During the probationary period (A), you can't (B) apply for any leaves. (C)

970. The poor student had (A) to learn the essay by heart (B) before the examination. (C)

971. What was shown (A) in the advertisement (B) is entirely different from this. (C)

972. The government could not (A) sanction money earlier (B) due to lake of fund. (C)

973. A five days tour (A) has been arranged (B) for the NSS students of our college. (C)

974. Shall we discuss about (A) this matter tomorrow, as (B) it is already late now ? (C)

975. Between Amit and Ajay, (A) the latter looks (B) more comfortable now, isn't it ? (C)

976. We invited our Secretary (A) to inaugurate formally (B) the Alumni Association. (C)

977. The children had been (A) playing in the hot sun (B) till there parents came. (C)

978. Why did you call (A) the third party whence (B) you could settle it yourselves ? (C)

979. Prof. Priya needs no (A) preparation as she (B) is very good at extempore .(C)

980. "What a fine piece (A) of art is this ?" (B) the tourist said to the guide. (C)

981. While preparing (A) the resume, he forgotted (B) to mention his experience. (C)

982. You will have to pay (A) the prize for all your (B) present misconduct. (C)

983. My uncle lives (B) in the third floor (B) of the decade old apartment . (C)

984. A five year's old (A) poor boy requested me (B) to buy him some food. (C)

985. The benefit of the suspicion (A) always goes (B) in favour of the batsman. (C)

986. We observe that (A) none of the three siblings (B) resembles one another. (C)

987. The women's Bill (A) was easily paused in the (B) floor of the House. (C)

988. There was no debates (A) over the money laundering (B) case against him. (C)

989. The former minister has (A) convicted of money (B) laundering and tax evasion. (C)

990. As Sudha is the soul (A) bread winner of the family,(B) we have to support her. (C)

991. We paid the lodge (A) an additional ten dollars (B) for the maintainance charges. (C)

992. He has denies (A) all the charges levelled against him (B) as if he was honest.(C)

993. He has no any company (A) with him due to (B) his mercurial temperament .(C)

994. Do you have some (A) books on (B) Artificial Intelligence and its origin ? (C)

995. Never distrust yours (A) friend since he is always (B) loyal, honest and reliable. (C)

996. Only then attending (A) this lecture, I could understand the nuances of English. (C)

997. The attendance of the (A) class was kept on the table (B) by mine friend. (C)

998. Don't disclose (A) your identity to any people (B) whoever you met here. (C)

999. It's up to you (A) to follow my advice or not, (B) as I can't compel to you . (C)

1000. The prayer session (A) was conducted by our Principal (B) as excellently as ever. (C)

Answers

901. c	902. b	903. a	904. a	905. a
906. c	907. c	908. a	909. b	910. a
911. b	912. b	913. c	914. a	915. c
916. c	917. c	918. a	919. d	920. c
921. b	922. a	923. a	924. a	925. a
926. a	927. b	928. b	929. c	930. d
931. c	932. a	933. a	934. d	935. b
936. b	937. d	938. a	939. c	940. d
941. c	942. c	943. b	944. a	945. b
946. b	947. b	948. a	949. b	950. b
951. c	952. d	953. b	954. b	955. d
956. a	957. a	958. d	959. d	960. b
961. a	962. c	963. c	964. d	965. c
966. b	967. b	968. b	969. c	970. d
971. c	972. c	973. a	974. a	975. c
976. b	977. c	978. b	979. d	980. b
981. b	982. b	983. b	984. a	985. a
986. d	987. b	988. a	989. a	990. a
991. c	992. a	993. a	994. a	995. a
996. a	997. c	998. c	999. c	1000.d

Your score now /100

ஆங்கில பயிற்சி

மதுரை, செப். 4 –

மதுரை மருத்துவக் கல்லூரியில் முதலாம் ஆண்டு மாணவ, மாணவியருக்கு, ஆங்கிலம் பேசுதல், இலக்கண பிழையின்றி எழுதுதல் உள்ளிட்டவை குறித்து மதுரைக் கல்லூரி ஆங்கில பேராசிரியர் வெங்கடேஷ் பயிற்சி அளித்தார்.

மேலும் ஆங்கில வாசிப்பு முக்கியத்துவம் பற்றி பேசினர்.

எளிதில் கற்கும் வகையில் நூல் வெளியிடப்பட்டது.

பேராசிரியர்கள் சோபனா, ஜெயந்தி மற்றும் பலர் கலந்து கொண்டனர்.

Dinamalar, Sep'4 2023

Award for professor

S. Venkatesh, Associate Professor of English, The Madura College, received the 'Most Innovative Educationist ' award in Chennai on August 27. He is presently running a YouTube channel through which students are trained in vocabulary enrichment, phonetics, spotting the errors, nitty gritty of English grammar and so on. He has authored two books and the third is to be released on September 5, the Teachers' Day.

The Hindu, Sep'5 2023

The release of this book @ The Madura College, Madurai